Reviews for The Possessed & Other Books by Troy Taylor

D1520953

The Watseka Wonder is one of the most bizarre, mind-bending cases of possession on record. In his book, The Possessed, Troy Taylor artfully probes a mystery that will challenge your beliefs about spirits, possession and the afterlife. This amazing story is fascinating, logic-defying, emotional -- and all true!
ROSEMARY ELLEN GUILEY, Author of ENCYCLOPEDIA OF GHOSTS & SPIRITS

SO, THERE I WAS by Troy Taylor and Len Adams is not only a chilling look at the strange happenings and weird events that can occur during ghost tours and investigations, it s also one of the funniest books about the paranormal that has ever been written! Troy and Len (along with Luke Naliborski) present a hilarious, and often spooky, collection of stories from haunted places all over the country. You dont want to miss this one!
DAVID GOODWIN, author of GHOSTS OF JEFFERSON BARRACKS

Troy Taylors GHOST HUNTERS GUIDEBOOK is the best manual that you can find on the how-tos of ghost hunting and I highly recommend it to anyone who wants to get involved in the paranormal field and see what ghost hunting is all about. Troy presents it like it really is and is careful to let the reader know there is nothing glamorous about being a ghost hunter! He presents the methods, the equipment and the photos in a way that no one else has ever done. Dont miss out on this book!
KEITH AGE, Founder of the LOUISVILLE GHOST HUNTERS SOCIETY & Host of SPOOKED

Troy Taylor has done it yet again. In Haunted Illinois, the author has hit that rare (and delightful) middle ground between fascinating paranormal research and compelling storytelling. His stories will put you on the edge of your seat and his insights into the supernatural will keep you there. A rare and delightful find and a must-read from one of the best ghost authors writing today.
MARK MARIMEN, author of the HAUNTED INDIANA Series

Ghost Books by Troy Taylor

HAUNTED ILLINOIS BOOKS
Haunted Illinois (1999 / 2001 / 2004)
Haunted Decatur (1995)
More Haunted Decatur (1996)
Ghosts of Millikin (1996 / 2001)
Where the Dead Walk (1997 / 2002)
Dark Harvest (1997)
Haunted Decatur Revisited (2000)
Flickering Images (2001)
Haunted Decatur: 13th Anniversary Edition (2006)
Haunted Alton (2000 / 2003)
Haunted Chicago (2003)
The Haunted President (2005)
Mysterious Illinois (2005)
Dead Men Do Tell Tales: Bloody Chicago (2006)
Resurrection Mary (2007)
The Possessed (2007)

HAUNTED FIELD GUIDE BOOKS
The Ghost Hunters Guidebook (1997/ 1999 / 2001/ 2004 / 2007)
Confessions of a Ghost Hunter (2002)
Field Guide to Haunted Graveyards (2003)
Ghosts on Film (2005)
So, There I Was (with Len Adams) (2006)

HISTORY & HAUNTINGS SERIES
The Haunting of America (2001)
Into the Shadows (2002)
Down in the Darkness (2003)
Out Past the Campfire Light (2004)
Ghosts by Gaslight (2007)

OTHER GHOSTLY TITLES

Spirits of the Civil War (1999)
Season of the Witch (1999/ 2002)
Haunted New Orleans (2000)
Beyond the Grave (2001)
No Rest for the Wicked (2001)
Haunted St. Louis (2002)
The Devil Came to St. Louis (2006)

BARNES & NOBLE PRESS TITLES

Weird U.S. (Co-Author with Mark Moran & Mark Scuerman) (2004)
Weird Illinois (Barnes & Noble Press) (2005)
Weird Virginia (2007)
Haunting of America (2006)
Spirits of the Civil War (2007)
Into the Shadows (2007)

The Possessed

The History & Horror of the Watseka Wonder

By Troy Taylor

- A Dark Haven Entertainment Book from Whitechapel Press -

This book is dedicated to all of those readers who are as fascinated with the unsolved and the unknown as I am and those who continue seeking answers, even though they may be impossible to find.

Original Cover Artwork Designed by
Visit M & S Graphics at http://www.manyhorses.com

This Book is Published By:
Whitechapel Press
A Division of Dark Haven Entertainment, Inc.
15 Forest Knolls Estates - Decatur, Illinois - 62521
(217) 422-1002 / 1-888-GHOSTLY
Visit us on the internet at http://www.prairieghosts.com

First Printing -- October 2007
ISBN: 1-892523-55-8

Printed in the United States of America

The Possessed

The History & Horror of the Watseka Wonder

Thus, for ten months and ten days, did these phenomena continue to excite and agitate the people. The following is a true narrative...

Dr. E.W. Stevens

Lurancy had the memories, emotions, recognitions, physical nuances and personality of a person dead for twelve years. In most cases of multiple personality, the individual does not have this knowledge of the early life of another, sometimes fictitious, personality. It seems irrefutable that the spirit of a real person who had actually been born, grown, loved and died upon this earth had taken over the body of Lurancy Vennum.

Beth Scott & Michael Norman

The "Watseka Wonder" does not appear to be only a matter of dual personality. Observers were insistent that Lurancy's familiarity with the dead girl's life could not have been acquired by the usual means.

Robert Somerlott

Introduction

The story of the "Watseka Wonder," a phenomenon that occurred in the small Illinois town of Watseka in the late 1800s, still stands today as one of the most authentic cases of spirit possession in the history of America. It has been investigated, dissected and ridiculed but, as of this writing, no clear explanation for the events that took place has ever been offered. There are many theories that exist and yet there is not a single explanation that can encompass all of the strange happenings that are associated with this eerie case.

We have to accept the fact that we simply do not know as much about the unexplained as we think we do.

Throughout history, there have been a handful of paranormal cases that have managed to endure the test of time. They are incidents that have, no matter how many times they are written about and researched, remained elusive. Some of these cases include the Bell Witch haunting in Tennessee, Resurrection Mary on Chicago's southwest side, the St. Louis Exorcism and, of course, the Watseka Wonder. All of these cases have fascinated me since childhood and, in fact, I have written about all of them extensively, perhaps to try and purge my obsession for them.

I first became interested in the story of the Watseka Wonder when I was still in elementary school. I ran across it in one of those books of "true ghost stories" that always seemed to be offered to try and entice kids to read. I needed no convincing and was already an avid reader, spending most of my time devouring graphic material that was likely inappropriate for a child of my tender years. I became fascinated by the account of the young girl who was possessed by the spirit of another girl (this one dead) and tried to seek out anything else that I could find on the story. A search of the school library came up empty and I found nothing about the case at the public library either. This intrigued me even more but, unfortunately, it would years before I was able to track down anything more about Mary and Lurancy.

As my interest in the paranormal continued to grow and I became actively involved in researching and writing about other true mysteries, I began to find brief mentions of the Watseka Wonder in a few obscure books and in the writings of the Spiritualists and the investigators of the early 1900s. I also found that a novel about the case had been published in the 1970s and I became even more fascinated by this strange story.

Eventually, after much searching through old book listings and antiquarian bookstores, I made it back to the source of the story, the small booklet published by Dr. E. Winchester Stevens, who had documented the case at the time it occurred. This discovery would eventually lead me to the town of Watseka itself. I came to town as part of the cast for a documentary film called *Children of the Grave*, which featured hauntings connected to children. The story of the Watseka Wonder was a natural addition to the film. (As it turned out, the filming for the "Watseka Wonder" section of the film became so large that it was moved to the sequel, *Children of the Grave 2: The Possessed*.) The writers and directors, Christopher and Phillip Booth, were friends of mine and they, along with producer Keith Age, had asked me to be a part of the film and to talk about the Watseka

Wonder.

I'm sure that being part of the documentary opened many doors for all of us in town but I was still surprised to find so many people interested in, and willing to talk about, a controversial paranormal case that was more than a century old. The Iroquois County Historical Society was more than willing to open their building for us and the staff at the public library offered their time in making stacks of copies from their files. The current owners of the Vennum and Roff houses, Scott Anderson and John Whitman, never hesitated when they were asked if we could film there, interview them and basically camp out in their homes for the night. Even Watseka's mayor turned up to welcome us to town.

If I had any doubts about the story of the Watseka Wonder being just as real and just as relevant today as it was in the 1870s, then they were dashed with a single visit to the town where it all took place. The spirits of Mary Roff, and Lurancy Vennum still linger over Watseka and the mystery is still as puzzling as it was decades ago.

So, what really happened in the Watseka Wonder case? Was Lurancy Vennum really possessed by the spirit of Mary Roff? There are many who do not believe that she was, writing the entire incident off as a hoax, or to an early documented case of multiple personalities. There are others who did believe, including scores of people who were present at the time it was taking place. On June 1, 1878, the editor of the *Iroquois County Times* wrote:

There are yet numberless mysteries in this world, though science has dissipated many wonders and philosophy has made plain many marvels. There is much that is unaccountable in the actions of Spiritualistic mediums, and they do many things which puzzle the greatest philosophers. Skeptical and unbelieving as we are, and slight as our evidence has been, we have seen enough to convince us that Spiritualism is not all humbug. The case of Lurancy Vennum, a bright young girl of fourteen years, has been the subject of much discussion in Watseka during the past year, and there is a good deal in it beyond human comprehension…

There follows a short description of some of the facts in the case and the article continues:

Mr. and Mrs. A.B. Roff kindly offered to take charge of her until her mind would change and she would become herself again. She went there in February and remained until about three weeks ago; since then she has become 'Lurancy Vennum' and is healthy and full of intelligence. During her entire stay at Mr. Roff's she never failed to call Mr. Roff 'Father' and Mrs. Roff 'Mother,' and she often referred to matters and incidents which occurred during the life of Mary Roff, and which Mr. and Mrs. Roff and Mrs. Alter remembered well. Indeed, she mentioned so many things with which Mary Roff had been familiar and which she certainly had never heard of, that it was hard for even the most skeptical not to believe there was something supernatural about her. If she was not prompted by the spirit of Mary Roff, how could she know so much about the family, people with whom she was not acquainted and whom she had never visited?

Even then, many in Watseka were divided about the reality of the case. Many simply refused to believe it, or in some cases, their personal philosophies did not allow them to believe that such things were possible. The Vennums' minister, who believed Lurancy to be insane, told the family after the possession: "You should have placed her in the state asylum as I told you."

With that, I will ask again – what really happened in Watseka in 1878? The story of Lurancy Vennum and Mary Roff is one that has become filled with theories, legends and lies over the years and in many cases, it has become hard to separate what is fiction and what is fact.

However, with this book --- the first full-length book about the Watseka Wonder case (not counting the 1977 novel) that has been published since Dr. Steven's booklet in 1879 --- I hope to be able to separate the facts from the fancy and tell the story as it really happened. Can we actually solve a mystery that has proven to be unsolvable for nearly 130 years?

I can't promise to do that but I do think that I can provide enough information and enough evidence to allow readers to decide for themselves what they choose to believe, or not believe, about the case. My job here is not to decide the truthfulness of the story for you --- but to allow you to judge for yourself.

Good luck!

Troy Taylor
Summer 2007

I. Possessed by the Spirits

Even though the modern day idea of "possession" seems to involve demons, spinning heads and little girls levitating above beds, the concept of being possessed by spirits has actually been with us for centuries, long before the Devil and his minions became a part of our lore. Man has long been fascinated with the thought that a person's mind and soul can be taken over by spirits, whether those of the dead or even those of the gods.

The ancient Greeks, who maintained daily contact with their gods and worshipped them in a personal manner, believed that the deities manipulated the lives of mortals every day, either by causing them to act in a specific way or by simply taking over their bodies and using them to do their bidding. Followers of Buddhism and Hinduism attribute all kinds of everyday disturbances to possession by spirits and many African tribal religions teach that possession by gods and spirits show favor on man and offer proof of supernatural powers. In the Bible, events are recounted when Jesus exorcised "unclean spirits" during his ministry. There is nothing to say that these spirits were in league with the Devil but most Catholic theologians, and fundamentalist Christians, have come to believe this was the case.

And here lurks the dark side of possession.

As the Catholic Church began its rise to power, church officials denied the possibility that any sort of spirit possession could be anything other than the work of the Devil. The church became the greatest proponent of demonic possession and exorcism and remains connected with it to this day.

The state of "possession" is defined as the presence of a spirit entity that occupies and controls the physical body of the subject. The symptoms of such a possession can be many, depending on the type of possession you are dealing with. In cases of demonic possession, symptoms can include agonized convulsions, shouting of obscenities, vomiting, excessive violence, poltergeist-like events and even a state of unnatural calm.

A spirit possession is a completely different kind of situation. In such cases, the possession seems to be more mental than physical. Although subjects may sometimes do things and act out in ways they will not later remember, they appear to be themselves. It seems to be more of a case of having their mind taken over by the spirits than having their bodies commandeered.

In order to understand the events that are alleged to have occurred in Watseka in 1878, we have to take a closer look at the concept of possession, from its darkest elements to its contacts with the dead.

Demonic Possession

The idea of being possessed by demons is the most familiar of all types of possession to the modern reader. Thanks to movies, television shows and books about the supernatural, we have been deluged with accounts of horrific incidents like the 1949 St. Louis Exorcism (see my own book on the subject) and the 1928 exorcism that took place in Iowa.

Even demonic possession, though, has many faces. No unanimous opinion exists as to the cause, or causes, of demonic possession and the subject has involved such varied disciplines as religion, medicine, psychiatry, spiritualism and demonology. Many would dismiss the idea of demonic possession as fraud but it is clear that in many cases, the symptoms, sometimes of deep distress, mental or even physical torment, are genuine, no matter how controversial the cause. In spite of the reality of the symptoms, though, there is no denying that many subjects would be better served by the care of a psychiatrist rather than that of an exorcist.

To most doctors and mental health specialists, a diagnosis of "demonic possession" is one that reeks of medieval superstition and ignorance. The symptoms, they believe, have either a wide range of medical and psychiatric interpretations or can be dismissed as misperceptions and hallucinations. They feel that cases of possession in the past were nothing more than conditions like epilepsy, hysteria or what has been referred to as multiple personality disorder, which is rare in itself.

During a convulsive seizure, a person with epilepsy can experience extreme muscular rigidity, foaming at the mouth and rapid back and forth head movements. The face may be distorted and he or she may produce strange, guttural noises that are caused by a spasm of the throat muscles. During the period just before a seizure, the patient may experience hallucinations, either seeing or smelling things that aren't there or hearing weird sounds and voices.

These are all things that are sometimes attributed to people who are thought to be possessed but there are also additional symptoms that strike genuine victims of demonic possession that cannot be dismissed as epilepsy. The first of these is that a demonic attack may last for hours at a time, as opposed to the five minutes or so that an epileptic seizure usually lasts. Extreme movements, rather than rigidity, are more characteristic to a possessed person and muscular reflexes tend to be strong. According to church records, other signs of a possession include "the ability to speak with some familiarity in a strange tongue or to understand it when spoken by another; the faculty of divulging future and hidden events; and the display of powers which are beyond the subject's age and natural condition."

A condition called "hysteria" also produces many of the

symptoms of someone who is possessed. In such cases, victims will scream and cry out and their body will go through will gyrations or will be almost motionless. At times, their bodies can also bend backwards into a semi-circle shape as their heads are thrown back and forth with great violence. In many cases, those suffering from demonic possession will act in much the same manner. The bending of the body is mentioned in many writings and case studies on demonic possession.

Given this partial duplication of symptoms, how does the church distinguish between hysteria and genuine cases of possession? The determining factor is the context in which the symptoms occur. If they come about at the same time as an aversion to religious objects, and if they are accompanied by paranormal phenomena (the ability to detect religious items that have been hidden, understand languages never learned, levitation, and so on), the church is much more likely to consider the symptoms to be manifestations of demonic possession.

In opposition to the ideas of the church, modern science it quick to try and explain away the idea of demonic (or spiritual) possession. There are many possible explanations as to why a person cannot be possessed and yet, with each of the explanations, none of them contains all of the symptoms that a possessed person is alleged to exhibit. Does this mean that possession can be real --- or is it simply that science has not yet found a reason as to why some so-called "demonic possessions" defy explanation?

One thing is certain, whether demonic possession is real or not, there are people all over the world who believe in it --- and they have whole-heartedly believed this for centuries. The belief dates back to the early Catholic Church but it gained prominence due to a number of famous cases during the Middle Ages. Instances of nuns possessed by satanic influences affected convents in France, Italy, Spain, Germany and elsewhere. Commonly beginning with a single nun, the possession proved to be highly contagious and whole groups became involved. Coinciding with the relentless years of the Spanish

Exorcism of demons dates back hundreds of years for the Catholic Church

Inquisition, the cases often had tragic consequences for anyone who might be accused of causing a person to become possessed. Usually the victims themselves were not considered to be responsible for what had occurred to them and their treatment was confined to the expulsion of the demons by exorcism. The exorcists, who formed one of the minor orders of the Church, were priests who specialized in the work using methods that had been drawn out in the *Rituale Romanum.*

The *Rituale Romanum,* which is still used in the Roman Catholic Church today, was issued in 1614 at the behest of Pope Paul V. It was designed to formalize practices that had developed during the early days of the Christian Church and it placed special emphasis on identifying diabolical possession, selection of the exorcist and defining the setting and texts to be used during an exorcism ritual. The ritual has retained its central features over the past centuries, although recent revisions were made in 1952 and 1999. Today, the text is initially designed to establish the actual presence of demonic possession. For this, the text specifies:

First of all, one should not easily assume that someone is possessed by a demon unless he shows signs that distinguish the possessed person from those who suffer from melancholy [mental illness] or some [physical] disease. The signs indicating the presence of a possessed person are as follows: speaking in an unknown tongue or understanding someone who speaks in a language unknown to the person; revelation of distant and unknown matters; manifestation of powers beyond one's natural age and condition; as well as other such matters, all of which, when taken together, compound such indications.

However, as noted by Monsignor Carlo Balducci in 1959, parapsychology has widened the possibility of natural phenomena (such as psychokinesis and precognition) being interpreted as demonic in origin. Combine that with mental illness and medical conditions and it becomes much harder to determine what is a real demonic possession and what is not. For this reason, the exorcist's first task was to confirm that the victim was indeed possessed by a Christian devil, who existed only by the permission of God. In that way, the demon was subject to the authority of the Christian priest. Numerous manuals covered not only the discovery and expulsion of demons from humans and animals but many techniques for countering demonic offenses, both small and large. There was, it was believed in the past, scarcely any evil that a demon was not capable of, from the drying up of milk cows to the more serious grievance of inhibiting the sexual intercourse of married couples.

From the records, it is clear that an exorcism had the nature of a contest between the exorcist, armed with the authority of God and the Church, and the demonic intruder. An exorcist could fail, he could even be destroyed if the battle went against him and the fact that several exorcists died prematurely ---- and several went insane --- seems to lend credence to the horror of the exorcism itself. The prayers, adjurations and commands of the exorcist, along with the ritual acts prescribed, were in themselves dramatic and when they provoked, as they were intended to do, a dialogue between the exorcist and the demon, they could be overwhelming and fantastic. For it was here that the drama of the confrontation reached its height as the demon's bestial voice belched out its obscenities and the priest's voice answered with commands and prayers.

While we think of an exorcism as "driving out" the demon, it is really more of a case of placing the demon on oath. In some instances, there may be more than one demon possessing a person. The word "exorcism" is derived from the Greek "ek" with the verb "horkizo," which means "I cause [someone] to swear" and refers to "putting the spirit or demon on oath." To put it simply, it means invoking a higher authority to bind the entity in order to control it and command it to act contrary to its own will. In the Christian sense, this higher authority is Jesus Christ, based on the belief that demons and evil spirits are afraid of Christ. This belief hearkens back to the story mentioned earlier when Jesus cast out a legion of devils from an afflicted man. And not only did Christ exorcize demons and unclean spirits but he gave the power to his disciples as well. "….He gave them power against unclean spirits, to cast them out, and to heal all manners of sickness, and all manner of disease." (Book of Matthew)

The greatest danger to the exorcist during the ritual is becoming possessed by the demon himself. This is the reason why the exorcist must be as free from sin as possible and to feel no secret need for punishment. Many priests will fast and pray for some time before taking part in the ritual and during a prolonged

Jesus exorcizes 'unclean spirits' from the body of a man in the biblical Book of Matthew

exorcism, while they continue to fast, some will report extreme weight loss. Only a priest who is convinced that he is right with God can be safe during an exorcism. Otherwise, the demon can easily entrap him.

The exorcism can last for days, or even weeks, physically draining everyone involved. It can also be a confusing and complicated series of events, all of which hopefully lead to success on the part of the exorcist. But is this success, when it does occur, really an expulsion of demonic spirits? Or could the successful exorcism be nothing more than a "spiritual placebo" that convinces the victim that whatever was plaguing him has departed? Many believe this to be the case and are often torn between the danger of playing into the delusions of a mentally ill person and the idea that whatever helps them must be a good thing.

Can exorcisms be dangerous? The answer seems to be "yes," to both the victim and the exorcist. But how dangerous can the ritual be? No one seems prepared to answer that but one thing is certain, the ritual is more cautiously employed by the Catholic Church today than it was in the past. When reviewing the conditions for demonic possession, there are many who dismiss them as nothing more than schizophrenia and other psychological disorders. For this reason, priests are cautioned to be as certain as possible that the person is truly demonically possessed before performing the ritual. In the Catholic Church, an exorcist must have the express permission of the archdiocese before beginning the ritual.

Exorcisms are not, and have not been for the past century or so, something to be entered into lightly.

Possession by the Holy Spirit

In direct opposition to the idea of being possessed by evil spirits, there are many facets of American culture and religion that believe man can be possessed by a divine spirit instead. This type of religious belief is called Pentecostalism and it is a sect of the Christian church that places special emphasis on the direct experience of God through

A Pentecostal church service includes music, prayer, laying on of hands (as shown above) and sessions of speaking in tongues. Believers are convinced that this is evidence of possession by the Holy Spirit

the baptism of the Holy Spirit. After the crucifixion and resurrection of Jesus, the Bible tells of what happened to his followers on the first day of Pentecost (a date that is seven days after Passover in the Jewish calendar). While gathered together, the apostles became possessed by the Holy Spirit. The Book of Acts described how small flames appeared above their heads and how each of them spoke in languages that were previously unknown to them.

The idea of "speaking in tongues" (glossolalia) became a basic tenet in Pentecostalism and it is still widely practiced today. There are several different types of the Pentecostal faith but the most conservative are members of the Apostolic branch, who are separated from many of the other "charismatic" churches. The Apostolic

Christians believe that a possession by the Holy Spirit is essential to salvation. They also believe that woman should only wear skirts and dresses, should not cut their hair, should not wear makeup or jewelry and that men should always wear their hair short, should abstain from facial hair and should always wear pants, never shorts. They also believe in what is called the "Oneness" doctrine, literally accepting the biblical instruction that all baptisms, healings and prayers should be in the name of "Jesus" only, not "in the name of the Father, Son and Holy Ghost," as most other churches believe.

Apostolic churches can be very lively, placing great emphasis on testifying, praise for the Lord, fiery sermons, and almost hypnotic music. It is during these music and prayer sessions that members of the congregation become possessed by the spirit, which can result in speaking in tongues, dancing, jumping up down, running through the church, shouting, crying, falling to the ground and passing out. I have personally witnessed some of these sessions and they can be both bizarre and a little frightening, too.

In extreme cases, divine spirit possession can even lead to handling snakes and drinking poison. Sects who take part in such behavior draw their inspiration directly from the Bible: "And these signs shall follow them that believe; In my name shall they cast out devils; they shall speak with new tongues; They shall take up serpents; and if they drink any deadly thing, it shall

In extreme cases of Holy Spirit possession, some believers handle snakes as evidence of divine protection.

not hurt them; they shall lay hands on the sick, and they shall recover." (Book of Mark)

The Pentecostal sect can trace its beginning back to the day of Pentecost and the 120 believers who were possessed by the spirit after Christ's ascension to heaven. In more recent times, the church as we know it today was formed. There were several incidents that occurred around the turn of the last century that led to the formation of the modern movement. The pivotal event occurred in 1901 when a woman named Agnes Ozman began speaking in tongues during a prayer meeting at Charles Fox Parham's Bethel Bible College in Topeka, Kansas. Parham, a minister with a Methodist background, created the doctrine that speaking in tongues was the "Bible evidence" of possession by the Holy Spirit. In addition, he cited the experience of the gathered disciples of Jesus on the day of Pentecost and the instructions of Peter in the Book of Acts as justification for their practices. The biblical reference stated: "Repent and be baptized, every one of you, in the name of Jesus Christ for the forgiveness of your sins. And you will receive the gift of the Holy Spirit." (Book of Acts)

Parham soon left Topeka and started a revival meeting ministry. The next significant (and controversial) event in Pentecostal history took place at the Azusa Street Revival in California. This revival was conducted by a student of Parham, an African-American man named William J. Seymour. Parham taught Seymour in Houston, Texas, but since Seymour was black, he was only allowed to sit outside the room and listen to Parham speak. Despite the racial segregation of the time, the Apostolic movement was largely accepting of African Americans and welcomed them into the church. This is significant due to the fact that it would be a black man who would launch the watershed event of the Pentecostal movement.

Speaking in tongues was already occurring in churches across the country by 1906, but the Azusa Street Revival would be the event that would make the movement known across the country. It began on April 9, 1906 in Los Angeles, at the home of Edward Lee, who claimed

The Azusa Street Mission in 1906. The revival here lasted for three years and gave birth to the Pentecostal Movement

that he had been possessed by the Holy Spirit. William Seymour claimed that he was possessed a few days later, on April 12. On April 18, the *Los Angeles Times* ran a front page story on the revival, "Weird Babel of Tongues, New Sect of fanatics is breaking loose, Wild scene last night on Azusa Street, gurgle of wordless talk by a sister".

By the third week of April, the small but growing congregation rented an abandoned African Methodist Episcopal Church at 312 Azusa Street and subsequently became organized as the Apostolic Faith Mission. They would go on to achieve national fame and today, almost all Pentecostal denominations can trace their historic roots to Azusa Street.

Pentecostalism, like any other major movement, has given birth to a large number of denominations, churches, separatists and even cults with a variety of differences between them. It is a faith that is outside of the norm and even its inception was counter-cultural to the social and political feelings of the time. Record numbers of African Americans and women, both black and white, were the initial leaders. As the Azusa Street Revival began to wane, doctrinal differences, as well as pressure from social, cultural and political events of the time, took their toll on the membership.

As a result, major divisions, separation and even the increase of extremism became apparent. Not wishing to affiliate with the Assemblies of God, formed in 1914, a group of ministers from predominantly white churches formed the Pentecostal Church of God in Chicago in 1919. George Went Hensley, a preacher who had left the Church of God in Cleveland, Tennessee, when it stopped embracing the practice of snake handling, is credited with starting the first church dedicated to this extreme practice in the 1920s. Taking up serpents, as it was called, was widely practiced in the poor, rural areas of the Appalachians. In African American communities of the 1940s, there were Father Divine with his Peace Mission and Daddy Grace, both claiming divinity, encouraging their followers to practice the wildest forms of Pentecostalism, which many referred to as "ecstaticism." This involved manic music, dancing, shouting and an almost ritual-like session that was meant to invite possession by the Holy Spirit.

No matter what doctrines divide the Pentecostal churches, spirit possession, and speaking in tongues as evidence of it, remains a staple. Members of the Apostolic sect believe that a "baptism" by the spirit is an actual event where the person is "filled up," causing them to utter words in languages that they should not know. Critics maintain that many of these "spirit utterances" are nothing more than nonsense words and gibberish, but those who experience a possession maintain that this is a very real religious experience.

Mounted by the Gods
Spirit Possession Around the World

As with Apostolic Pentecostals, contact with the spirits serves as the centerpiece of religious worship for many cultures around the globe. The main difference would be that in these other cultures, it is not the Holy Spirit that people are inviting into their bodies, but various other spirits and deities. Possession by a god shows the possessed person to be worthy of that god's attention and protection. For this reason, they believe that even minor accomplishments and problems come directly from the intervention of the gods.

In India, spirit possession is a part of everyday life. In most cases, the possessed are women, who attribute personal problems --- menstrual pain, inability to conceive a child, miscarriage, death of children, marital problems, abuse, a husband's infidelity --- to attacks by evil spirits. They are often put through an exorcism by a shaman whose techniques include blowing cow manure smoke at them, pressing rock salt between their fingers, beating the victim and pulling their hair, using copper coins and candy as presents to the spirit and, of course, reciting various prayers and mantras.

Besides being female, most of these victims come from the lower classes. Possession gives these people stature and even gains them a better place in society. At the least, a placation of these gods and demons usually involves showering gifts on the victims and the promise of better behavior from their friends, husbands and employers.

Although the people of Islam worship one god, Allah, they acknowledge the problems caused by minor spirits like *djinns* (genies). These spirits possess their victims, usually women, and cause sickness, martial discord and rebellious behavior. They will only depart if they are placated by gifts of food, clothing, liquor, jewelry or other presents for the possessed victims. At times, that also promise to leave if the men in the victim's life start treating them better. In this case, too, we can see how "possession by spirits" can cause the life of the victim to improve for the better!

Perhaps the best-known religious experience in which worshippers literally invite the gods and spirits into their body occurs in the practice of Voodoo (or Voudon). This faith is a traditional West African religion of faith and ritual practices that made its way to the New World with the importation of slaves several centuries ago. The core functions of Voodoo are to explain the forces of the universe, influence those forces and change human behavior. It is not an evil faith, as some misconceptions would have it, but one that is based in magical rituals and a large pantheon of gods.

During Voodoo ceremonies, believers are possessed by the gods

The number of gods within the bounds of Voodoo is large and quite complex. There are dozens of male and female gods that are related to natural phenomena and to historic and mythical individuals, as well as scores of ethnic gods that are defenders of certain clans or tribes. Some of the major gods include Legba, who takes the form of a snake, Mami Wata, who rules the water, Sakpata, who governs diseases and Baron Samedi, the lord of the dead.

Voodoo first appeared in the Americas in Santo Domingo (modern-day Haiti) where slaves were documented devoting rituals to the power of nature and the spirits of the dead. For many enslaved Africans, such spiritual traditions provided a means of emotional and spiritual resistance to the hardships of their lives. In time, slaves from the Caribbean were brought to America and they brought their practice of Voodoo with them.

The first American reference to Voodoo in official documents can be found in New Orleans during the Spanish regime in 1782. In a document that tells of imports to the colony, there is a terse line regarding black slaves that have been brought from the island of Martinique. The Spanish governor, Galvez, states: "These negroes are too much given to voodooism and makes the lives of the citizens unsafe." Galvez was a soldier and was not a man of superstition, but he made an attempt to ban the importation of slaves from the Caribbean for a time for a very good reason --- he feared for the lives of the colonists. Around this same time (and again in 1804), a slave revolt had rocked the island of Haiti. The revolt was based around the practice of Voodoo and would eventually end with the French being driven from the island. Many of the French escaped to New Orleans and brought their slaves with them. Tensions simmered in the city with the arrival of more Voodoo-practicing slaves.

From the beginnings of the New Orleans colony in 1718, the white colonists had been troubled by the beliefs of their slaves. Shiploads of captives came through the city on a regular basis and were bought and sold for manual labor and household work. Thousands of them were brought by ship from Africa, packed into ships and treated like animals. There were caged and either "tamed," or killed, before being sold at auction.

These slaves, most of whom spoke no French, brought their religions, charms and spells with them from Africa, but they soon learned that they were forbidden to practice their own religions by their new masters. Many of them were baptized into the Catholic Church and later, the use of Catholic icons would play a major role in Voodoo. The church's icons would take their place in Voodoo hierarchy and be worshipped as if the slaves were offered prayers to the saints of the Catholic Church. The saints became "stand-ins" for important Voodoo deities. Even today, statues, candles and icons depict various Catholic images that are Voodoo symbols, as well. In this way, Voodoo became firmly entrenched in the culture of New Orleans and other regions of the American South.

One of the primary traditions of Voodoo involves the possession of the faithful by the gods to obtain true communion and protection.

During Voodoo ceremonies, worshippers are overcome by the chanting, dancing and pounding drums and are "mounted" by the gods, becoming the god's own "horse." During this event, they take on the personal characteristics of the god, such as the god's preference of food, perfumes and drink; their patterns of speech; use of profanity; and even a penchant for smoking large cigars, a common Voodoo tradition.

While possessed, the worshipper may endure great extremes of heat and cold, suffer cuts and bruises with no pain, dance for hours at a time, tear the heads off live chickens that are used for blood sacrifices and even engage in ritual sex with others who are possessed. They may also issue prophecies and announcements about local affairs and while the word of the spirits is not always taken seriously, there is little doubt that the events that are occurring are real. As far as the other worshippers are concerned, the possessed person has literally become the deity and is accorded all rights and honors that would be granted to the god. Once the possession ends, though, no special treatment is given to that person. At the next ceremony, the same god is likely to simply possess someone else and the honor moves on to the next person.

Spiritualism
Inviting in the Dead

We cannot underestimate the role that the practice of Spiritualism played in the story of the Watseka Wonder. For one thing, the story would have never have been as widely publicized as it was without the Spiritualist press and it's also unlikely that it would have never been documented and investigated in the manner that it was if not for the Spiritualists. Of course, the involvement of the Spiritualists would be both a blessing and as curse for the case as some would later claim that the incident might never have happened at all if not for the meddling of Dr. Stevens, a avowed practitioner of the faith.

Spiritualism was a movement that was founded with the idea that the dead can, and do, communicate with the living. It was invented in American in 1848, which seems rather fitting. Historians are often fond of remarking that America has, throughout its relatively short history, been a nation of extremes. Whether it's for the best or not, America has often been host to strong passions and great enthusiasms. They range from the vicious hysteria of the lynch mob to the ecstasies of the religious revival meeting and cover everything in between. Nowhere is this great passion as evident as it is in the history of Spiritualism. The movement swept the country, even in those days before radio, television and mass communication. People became obsessed with this alleged ability to communicate with the dead and even the most conservative, uneducated and average people became part of the new movement.

Although the idea that man was able to communicate with spirits had existed already for centuries, modern belief in such a practice came about in March 1848 in Hydesville, New York. The Spiritualist movement would remain strong for nearly a century, enjoying its greatest revival after the Civil War and again after World War I.

A dramatic rendering of the night when the Fox sisters confronted the entity in the cottage and coaxed it into communicating with them.

The events that led to the founding of Spiritualism began in a cottage rented by the Fox family. John Fox and his wife had two young daughters, Margaret and Kate, and they settled temporarily into the cottage. Fox was a farmer who had come to New York from Canada and had purchased land nearby. A home was being built on the new property and he moved his family into the cottage until the other house could be completed. Their stay would turn out to be very eventful.

Within days of moving in, the noises began. The banging and rattling sounds pounded loudly each night, disturbing them all from their sleep. At first, John Fox thought nothing of the sounds that his wife and children reported and were so frightened by. He assumed that they were merely the usual noises of an unfamiliar dwelling, amplified by active imaginations. Soon, however, the reports took another turn. Kate woke up screaming one night, saying a cold hand had touched her on the face. Margaret swore that rough, invisible fists had pulled the blankets from her bed. Even Mrs. Fox swore that she had heard disembodied footsteps walking through the house and then going down the wooden steps into the dank cellar.

Fox, not a superstitious man, was perplexed. He tried walking about the house, searching for squeaks and knocks in the floorboards and along the walls. He tested the windows and doors to see if vibrations in the frames might account for the sounds. He could find no explanation for the weird noises and his daughters became convinced that the house had a ghost. According to local stories, the house was haunted long before the Fox family moved in. Legend had it that a traveling peddler had been murdered there and his body buried in the basement. John Fox dismissed this as nothing more than nonsense --- and yet he could find no explanation for the strange events.

On the evening of March 31, Fox began his almost nightly ritual of exploring the house for the source of the sounds. The tapping had begun with the setting of the sun and although he searched the place over and over again, he was no closer to a solution. Then, Kate began to realize that whenever her father knocked on a wall or doorframe, the same number of inexplicable knocks would come in reply. It was as if someone, or something, was trying to communicate with them.

Finding her nerve, Kate spoke up, addressing the unseen presence by the nickname that she and her sister had given it. She called out, "Here, Mr. Splitfoot! Do as I do!"

She clapped her hands together two times and seconds later, two knocks came in reply, seemingly from inside the wall. She followed this display by rapping on the table and the precise number of knocks came again from the unseen presence. The activity caught the attention of the rest of the family and they entered the room with Kate and her father. Mrs. Fox tried asking aloud questions of fact, such as the ages of her daughters and the age of a Fox child who had earlier passed away. To her surprise, each reply was eerily accurate.

Unsure of what to do, John Fox summoned several neighbors to the house to observe the phenomenon. Most of them were very skeptical, but they were soon astounded to find their ages and various dates and years given in response to the questions they asked.

One neighbor, and a former tenant in the house, William Duesler, decided to try and communicate with the source of the sounds in a more scientific manner. He asked repeated questions and was able to create a form of alphabet using a series of knocks. He also was able to determine the number of knocks that could be interpreted as "yes" and "no." In such a manner, he was able to identify the subject of the disturbances. The secret of the haunting came out, not in private, but before an assembled group of witnesses. The presence in the house claimed that it was the spirit of the peddler who had been murdered and robbed there years before.

The once eerie, but entertaining, evening now took on a more sinister tone. John Fox and William Duesler went down to the basement and began to dig. After more than an hour, they had little to show for their trouble but an empty hole and sore backs. Then Fox noticed something odd beneath the blade of his shovel. He prodded at the object and then picked it up. It appeared to be a small piece of bone with a few strands of hair still clinging to it. Spurred on by the gruesome discovery, he and Duesler began to dig once more. They found a few scraps and tatters of clothing, but little else. They were far from disappointed though, as a local doctor determined that the bone appeared to be a piece of a human skull. They were convinced that the presence in the house was indeed the ghost of the luckless peddler!

Shortly afterwards, the story of the Fox family took a more dramatic turn. The two daughters were both purported to have mediumistic powers and the news of the unearthly communications with the spirit quickly spread. By November 1849, they were both giving public performances of their skills and the Spiritualist movement was born. The mania to communicate with the dead swept the country and the Fox sisters became famous.

Over the years, the credibility of the Fox family was called into question. As no real evidence existed that a peddler was killed in the house, many accused the family of making up the entire story to support their claims of supernatural powers. It may come as no surprise to the reader that the Spiritualist movement was riddled with fraud, but was the story of the murdered peddler merely a ruse to prove the powers of the Fox sisters?

It's possible that Margaret and Kate, had they not died years before, would have been vindicated in 1904. By this time, their former home had been deserted for some years. A group of children were playing in the ruins one day when the east wall of the cellar collapsed, nearly killing one of them. A man who came to their aid quickly realized the reason for the wall's collapse. Apparently, it had been a false partition, hastily and poorly constructed. Lying between the false brick wall and the genuine wall of the cellar were the crumbling bones of a man and a large box that was just like the ones that had been carried by peddlers a few decades before. A portion of the man's skull was missing.

Dead men, as they say, really do tell tales.

Or do they? That's been the mystery behind Spiritualism since it was first conceived. Were those involved with the movement really communicating with the dead? Skeptics, even of those times, were convinced they were not, but the public was not so easily

Spiritualist séances became a popular pastime in the late 1800s with mediums literally inviting the spirits of the dead to possess their bodies.

discouraged. In fact, they were fascinated with the reports coming from New York. News of these "spirited communications" quickly spread and the Fox Sisters became known all over the world. By November 1849, the girls were giving public demonstrations of their powers in contacting the spirit world and drawing crowds that numbered into the thousands. Seemingly overnight, Spiritualism became a full-blown religious movement, complete with scores of followers, its own unique brand of phenomena and codes of conduct for everything from spirit communication to séances.

The Spiritualists believed that the dead could communicate through what were called "mediums." They were sensitive persons who were in touch with the next world and while in a trance, they could pass along messages from the other side. Beside these "message mediums," there were also practitioners who could produce physical phenomena that was said to be the work of the spirits. These phenomena included lights, unearthly music, levitating objects, disembodied voices and even apparitions.

All of this was produced during what were called "séances" (or sittings), which were regarded as the most exciting method of spirit communication. Any number of people could attend and the rooms where the séances took place often contained a large table that the attendees could sit around, smaller tables that were suitable for lifting and tilting, and a cabinet where the mediums could be sequestered while the spirits materialized and performed their tricks. The sessions reportedly boasted a variety of phenomena, including musical instruments that played by themselves and sometimes flew about the room, glowing images, ghostly hands and messages from the dead.

While each séance was different, most had one thing in common in that they were always held in dark or dimly lighted rooms. Believers explained that the darkness provided less of a distraction to the audience and to the medium. They also added that since much of the spirit phenomena were luminous, they were much easier seen in the darkness. Those who were not convinced of the validity of the movement offered another explanation. They believed the dark rooms concealed the practice of fraud. Such allegations caused much in the way of controversy for the Spiritualist movement, as would later be evidenced in the case of the Watseka Wonder.

But while the Spiritualist movement brought the study of ghosts and spirits into the public eye, it also provided fame (and sometimes infamy) to many of those involved. Not only did the mediums gain notoriety, so did many of the investigators, and in many cases, the movement led to their ruin. Even the Fox Sisters, who had known such early fame and fortune, drank themselves to death and died penniless.

The downfalls of many of the mediums came about because of their exposure as fakes. It was obvious that Spiritualism was riddled with cases of deliberate fraud. It seemed easy to fool the thousands of people who were looking for a miracle and many of the mediums began lining their pockets with money they had swindled from naive clients.

Of course, that's not to say that all of the Spiritualists were dishonest. Many of them, like Sir Arthur Conan Doyle, creator of Sherlock Holmes, truly believed in the validity of the movement. At the very worst, many of these believers were good-hearted but gullible and at best, well -- there remain a few of the mediums for which no logical explanations have been suggested. For as William James said about the medium Lenora Piper... "to upset the conclusion that all crows are black, there is no need to seek demonstration that no crows are black; it is sufficient to produce one white crow; a single one is sufficient." Piper, James believed, was the "one white crow."

Interestingly, Spiritualism was never meant to turn into a faith or religious movement. It was little more than a popular pastime at first and the idea of communicating with the spirits was an amusing way to spend a long winter evening. There were a couple of factors that worked independently to cause Spiritualism to be inflated in importance and to be accepted as an actual religious faith. One of these was the rise of the Apostolic Church in America. The idea of speaking in tongues and being taken over by the Holy Spirit appealed to many and the Pentecostal faith (and its many offshoots) is still going strong today. Despite the fact that many ministers condemned Spiritualism as the "work of the Devil," it was not a far stretch for many to accept the possibility of strange events surrounding spirit communication and religious fervor at the same time.

Spiritualism saw a huge increase in popularity after the Civil War when many survivors fervently hoped to communicate with their war dead, and then, after a slow period, saw another resurgence after World War I. Most credit this to the wholesale slaughter of thousands of men on a scale the world had never seen before. Now, thanks to Spiritualism, bereaved families had hope that their lost loved ones were no longer lost at all. They could be contacted as if they were still alive. Spiritualism managed to fill a huge void for the everyday person, who now had something to cling to and a belief that their friends and family members had gone on to a better place.

By the early years of the 1900s, Spiritualism had largely died out as a popular movement, as it had never really been organized enough to continue, thanks to dissension in the ranks and internal politics among the leaders. The exposure of many frauds also took their toll and with science not being forthcoming about legitimizing the proof of Spiritualistic tenets, the movement began to fall apart. A little more than a decade later, though, World War I brought thousands of the bereaved back to séances when the movement went through its second heyday. Public interest soon cooled again and by the 1930s, the era of the physical medium was gone. Most agree that this period was largely killed off by the continued attacks by magicians and debunkers, who exposed fraud after fraud and gave even the legitimate practitioners a bad name. Soon, the mediums no longer wanted to expose themselves to scrutiny and so they abandoned the physical effects of flying trumpets and spirit materializations and turned to mental mediumship instead, which is more along the lines of spirit possession.

This type of mediumship involves inviting the spirits of the dead to take possession of the medium's body and pass along knowledge from the other side. There have been a number of famous incidents, involving this type of mediumship and some feel that this type of possession is exactly what occurred with Lurancy Vennum and the spirit of Mary Roff. Although many insist that it was not Lurancy who invited the spirit to enter her body, but rather some of the other, well-meaning protagonists in the case.

Aside from the Watseka Wonder, another famous --- and unsolved – case involving spirit possession was that of the Patience Worth, a mysterious being who took over the body of St. Louis housewife Pearl Curran.

Curran had little interest in the occult prior to 1913. She was born Pearl Leonore Pollard in Mound City, Illinois, in February 1883. She grew up in Texas, playing outdoors and exploring the countryside. Her parents, George and Mary, were easy-going and never really demanded much from Pearl, which probably made her an indifferent student. She left school after the eighth grade and began to study music in Chicago, where her uncle lived. She also played the piano at her uncle's Spiritualist church, where he was a medium. But Pearl and her parents were not Spiritualists and in fact, had no interest in the movement at all. Pearl had attended Sunday School as a child but few of the teachings stuck with her. She did not attend church and never read the Bible.

In fact, she rarely ever read anything at all. She had enjoyed books like *Black Beauty* and *Little Women* as a child and was always entertained by fairy tales but, probably thanks to her lack of education, she had little interest in literature or writing. Her only creative desires were to learn the piano and to perhaps act on stage, but she gave up that idea at 24 when she married John Curran.

Her marriage was as uneventful as her childhood had been. The Currans were not rich, but they did make a comfortable living. Pearl had a maid to take care of the household chores and she and her husband enjoyed going to restaurants and to the theater. They were a social couple and enjoyed visiting with friends and playing cards with neighbors in the evening. They seldom read anything, outside of the daily newspaper and some of the periodicals of the day, and never really had an opportunity to associate with well-educated writers or poets. They were happy and content in their middle-class home with their close friends and acquaintances. Never could they have imagined the changes that were coming to their lives.

In the afternoons, while their husbands were at work, Pearl would often have tea with her mother and with a neighbor named Mrs. Hutchings. It's likely that the Ouija board that was in the house on the afternoon of July 8, 1913 actually belonged to Mrs. Hutchings, who was curious about the contraption. Pearl had seen one of the boards before, and had even experimented with one at her uncle's home, but she professed to have no interest in them. In fact, she believed that Ouija boards were a boring and silly pastime. She had never seen the pointer spell out anything but gibberish.

Nevertheless, perhaps out of boredom, she agreed to play along that afternoon. To the ladies' surprise, the message on the board seemed to make sense. It spelled out: "Many moons ago I lived. Again I come. Patience Worth is my name."

The three women were startled. They certainly knew no one by that name. Who could Patience Worth have been? Pearl was the most skeptical of the three, doubting that the dead could make contact by way of a wooden board. However, at

Pearl Curran

her friend's urging, she asked the sender of the message to tell them something about herself. Replies to her queries began to come through the message board and were recorded by Pearl's mother. According to the spirit, who called herself Patience Worth, she had lived in Dorsetshire, England in either 1649 or 1694 (the planchette pointed to both dates) but even that information was difficult to obtain. Patience spoke in an archaic fashion, using words like "thee" and "thou" and sometimes refusing to answer their questions directly. When Mrs. Hutchings pushed for more information, the spirit first replied: "About me ye would know much. Yesterday is dead. Let thy mind rest as to the past." Eventually, though, the ladies would learn that Patience claimed to have emigrated to America, where she was murdered by Indians.

The initial contact with Patience Worth came through the Ouija board when Pearl and Mrs. Hutchings controlled it. But it was soon evident that Pearl was mainly responsible for the contact, for no matter who sat with her, the messages from Patience would come. The messages continued to be very strange in that whoever was speaking had an extensive knowledge of 17th century vernacular, and also of clothing, mechanical items, musical instruments and household articles of the period. One message stated: "A good wife keepeth the floor well sanded and rushes in plenty to burn. The pewter should reflect the fire's bright glow, but in thy day housewifery is a sorry trade."

Pearl was fascinated with the communication and began devoting more and more time to the Ouija board. Eventually, though, the messages began coming so fast that no one could write them down. Pearl suddenly realized that she didn't need the board anymore. The sentences were forming in her mind at the same time they were being spelled out on the board. She began to "dictate" the replies and messages from Patience to anyone who would write them. She would first employ a secretary, but later Pearl would record the words herself, using first a pencil and then a typewriter.

For the next 25 years, Patience Worth dictated a total of about 400,000 words. Her works were vast and consisted of not only personal messages, but creative writings as well. She passed along nearly 5,000 poems, a play, many short stories and several novels that were published to critical acclaim.

Shortly after Patience made her presence known, the Curran house in south St. Louis began to overflow with friends, neighbors and curiosity-seekers. When word reached the press, Casper Yost, the Sunday editor of the *St. Louis Post-Dispatch*, began publishing articles about Pearl Curran and the mysterious spirit who seemed to possess her. In 1915, he published a book called *Patience Worth, A Psychic Mystery* and the housewife from St. Louis became a national celebrity.

People came from all over the country and the Currans, always gracious and unpretentious, welcomed visitors who wanted to witness the automatic writings sessions where Pearl received information from Patience Worth. The Currans never charged any admission to the house and all of the writing sessions were conducted with openness and candor. There were no trappings of Spiritualism here with darkened rooms and candles. Pearl would usually just sit in a brightly lit room with her notebook or typewriter and when the messages began to come to her, she would begin to write.

Not surprisingly, many questioned the reality of the spectral Patience Worth and while she had her critics, she had her defenders as well. Witnesses were hard put to get Patience to offer much detail about her past. She seemed to think that her origins were unimportant, however she did mention landmarks and scenery around her former home in England. Newspaperman Casper Yost, who was one of the case's greatest defenders, took a trip abroad during the height of the phenomenon and when he reached Patience's alleged childhood home in Dorset he found the cliffs, old buildings, a monastery and scenery just as Patience had described them.

Perhaps the most convincing evidence that Patience Worth was not the conscious, or unconscious, creation of Pearl Curran is the material that she dictated for her books and stories. Patience seemed to be able to pass between old English dialects at will or could write in a semblance of modern English, as she did with most of her poetry.

The *Story of Telka* was one of her novels and it is a poetic drama of medieval life in rural England, written mostly in Anglo-Saxon words. It was composed during a series of sittings and as with other Patience Worth dictations, there were no revisions and no breaks where sentences left off and began again. The only comparable work to this novel is the Wickcliffe's Bible of the 14th Century, which is also composed of almost pure Anglo-Saxon. However, the language in *The Story of Telka* does not resemble the language in this particular Bible. In the novel, there are few words that the modern reader cannot understand, as if the desire by the writer was to create something that seemed old but could still be comprehended. Many argued that it would be impossible for a person living in turn-of-the-century St. Louis to create such a dramatic work and then limit the vocabulary to only easily understood words in an ancient form of their own language. It simply could not be done, they believed.

And this was far from Patience's only book. *The Sorry Tale* was a lengthy novel that was set in the time of Christ and in it, the author brought to life the Jews, Romans, Greeks and Arabs of the period. The book was also filled with an accurate knowledge of the political, social and religious conditions of the time. Critics hailed it as a masterpiece. It had been started on July 14, 1915 and two or three evenings a week were given over to the story until it was completed. The tale proceeded as fast as John Curran could take it down in abbreviated longhand and continued each night for as long as Pearl was physically able to receive it.

Professor W.T. Allison of the English Department of the University of Manitoba stated: "No book outside of the Bible gives such an intimate picture of the earthly life of Jesus and no book has ever thrown such a clear light upon the manner of life of Jews and Romans in the Palestine of the day of our Lord."

At the same time that *The Sorry Tale* was being produced, *The Merry Tale* was started as a relief from the sadness of the previous book. For a time, work was done on both novels during a single evening.

When the first words of the next book, *Hope Trueblood*, appeared, the sitters gathered at the Curran home were astonished. For the first time since Patience Worth's arrival, four years before, the material was in plain English. Her previous stories had dealt with ancient Rome, Palestine and Medieval England. This book told the story of a young girl's effort to find her family in Victorian England. When the book appeared in Great Britain, no clues were given as to its mysterious origins and reviewers accepted it as the work of a new and promising British author. Once critic stated: "The story is marked by strong individuality, and we should look with interest for further products of this author's pen."

While critics were impressed with the writing she produced, those who witnessed Pearl taking dictation from the spirit were even more astounded. For instance, *The Story of Telka*, which came in at over

70,000 words, was written over several sessions but was completed in just 35 hours. This type of speed was fairly typical, too. Once, in a single evening, 32 poems were delivered, along with several short stories. Sometimes in the course in one evening, Patience dictated portions of four novels, always resuming the work on each one at the same place she left off. Pearl took down all of the words, usually in the presence of a number of witnesses, and never made any revisions.

Those who came to investigate the strange events often made requests of Patience in order to test her. She never hesitated to respond to questions or tasks put to her. When asked to compose a poem on a certain subject, she would deliver the stanzas so quickly that they had to be taken down in shorthand. Weeks later, when asked to reproduce the poem, she could do so without any changes or errors. One night, psychic investigator Walter Franklin Prince, who was a regular visitor to the Curran house, posed an unusual task for Patience. Could she deliver a poem about the "folly of being an atheist" while simultaneously producing a dialogue that might take place between a wench and a jester at a medieval-era fair? He asked that she alternate the dialogue every two or three lines. Not only could Patience accomplish this, she did it so quickly that dictation was given to Pearl within eight seconds after the request was made. When she finished, Pearl stated that she felt as if her head had been squeezed in a steel vise.

It should come as no surprise to learn that Pearl Curran's life was permanently changed by the arrival of Patience Worth. While the alliance was undoubtedly a wondrous affair, as Pearl often stated, it also demanded a lot from her, both physically and mentally. She never allowed herself to become obsessed with Patience and the Currans never attempted to exploit the "partnership" for material gain. Pearl continued, with the help of her maid, to do all her own shopping, cooking and housework and she continued to visit with friends as she had always done. Two or three nights each week were set aside for writing sessions and Patience always dictated to Pearl, no matter how many people were in the house. She only stopped when startled by loud or sudden noises or when Pearl halted to converse with her guests.

Pearl explained that as the words flowed into her head, she would feel a pressure and then scenes and images would appear to her. She would see the details of each scene. If two characters were talking as they walked along a road, she would see the roadway, the grass on either side and perhaps the landscape in the distance. If they spoke a foreign language, she would hear them speaking but above them, she would hear the voice of Patience as she interpreted the speech and indicated what part of the dialogue she wanted in the story. She would sometimes even see herself in the scenes, standing as an onlooker or moving between the characters. The experience was so sharp and so vivid that she became familiar with things that she could have never have known about living in St. Louis. These items included lamps, jugs and cooking utensils used long ago in distant countries, types of clothing and jewelry word by people in other times and the sounds and smells of places that she had never even heard of before.

In spite of the visions and odd experiences, though, Pearl never went into a trance during the writing sessions. She understood the writing as it came and yet while calling out the words to the stenographer, she would smoke cigarettes, drink coffee and eat. She seemed always to be aware of her surroundings, no matter what else might be going on with her.

As time passed, Pearl was not completely satisfied with the literary reputation that was being achieved by Patience Worth. She became determined to take up writing herself, even though she had never written anything before and had never had the urge to do so. Unfortunately, her writings reflected her lack of education and talent. She wound up selling two of her stories to the *Saturday Evening Post*, but likely more for her fame as a conduit for Patience than for her own literary ability.

Patience was tolerant but condescending of her host's abilities, which may have been what prompted the love-hate relationship between them. Patience often scorned Pearl, but never failed to show her kindness. She simply seemed to think that her human counterpart was slightly stupid and that only by perseverance was she able to make herself known, especially when Pearl failed to grasp the spellings and meanings of certain words. But they plodded on together, continuing to amass a great body of work until about 1922.

In that year, the connection between the two of them began to deteriorate, possibly due to changes in Pearl's life and the fact that she had become pregnant for the first time at 39. After her husband and her mother both died, the contact between Patience and Pearl came less and less often and eventually it died away.

By this time, too, public interest in the mystery had faded, especially as no solution had ever been posed as to how the St. Louis housewife was accomplishing such remarkable feats. After the publication of several books and hundreds of poems, interest in Patience Worth vanished and cynicism replaced it. Debunkers accused Pearl of hiding her literary talent in order to exploit it in such a bizarre way and become famous. However, exhaustive studies have shown this to be highly unlikely, if not impossible. Scholars have analyzed Patience's works and have found them to accurate in historical detail and written in such a way that only someone with an intimate knowledge of the time could have created them.

Pearl Curran died in California on December 4, 1937. The *St. Louis Globe-Democrat* headlined her obituary with the words: "Patience Worth is Dead." And whatever the secret of the mysterious "ghost writer," it went to the grave with her.

What really happened in this case and why does it remain today one of our great unsolved mysteries? Was there actually an entity possessing Pearl from beyond the grave? Or could the writings have simply come from her unconscious mind?

No verification was ever made that Patience Worth actually lived in the 1600s and yet experts who studied Pearl Curran doubted that she could have produced the works attributed to the ghost on her own. She was a woman of limited education with no knowledge of the language used or the history and subject matter that was dictated by the alleged Patience Worth. Pearl simply could not have created the works of such literary quality.

Could the writings have come from her unconscious mind? Was Patience Worth a secondary personality of Pearl Curran? This also seems unlikely because for Pearl to have "created" a separate personality that was as vivid, colorful and rich as Patience Worth, she would have had to have some knowledge of the things that she was writing about, even if this knowledge had been an unconscious one. Those who have studied Pearl's past could discover, at no time, when she would have been exposed to the culture, people and languages of ancient times in Europe and the Middle East.

What did happen? Was it a true case of spirit possession and communication or one of the greatest hoaxes ever perpetrated on the literary and paranormal communities? It's unlikely that we will ever know for sure, but in the absence of any other explanation, we will have to leave this one in our stack of files on the "unexplained."

As mental mediumship progressed in the 1920s, new mediums came onto the scene and became nationally known figures. One of them, Arthur Ford, became famous for the possessions that he underwent by his spirit control, "Fletcher."

Ford never set out to become a medium. He was born into a Southern Baptist family in Titusville, Florida, in 1897. As a child, he had no profound psychic experiences. It wasn't until he was in the army as a young man that his psychic gifts began to emerge. In 1917, Ford had entered Transylvania College in Lexington, Kentucky, but found his studies interrupted by World War I. He joined the army in 1918 and became a second lieutenant, but he was never sent to the fighting overseas. Soon, he would start to realize that he had strange gifts that he was, at first, unable to understand.

At one point, during the deadly influenza epidemic at Camp Grant in Sheridan, Illinois, Ford dreamed the next day's death list. Then voices began to whisper to him the names of soldiers overseas who were soon killed in action. One night, Ford was startled awake by a vivid dream of his brother, George. He later learned that George became ill with influenza that same day and died a short time later.

When these strange visions and dreams began, Ford assumed that he was losing his mind. He returned to college, moody and depressed, but became acquainted with a psychology professor who made him realize that he was psychic, not insane, and Ford slowly began to develop his skills.

He graduated with a poor academic record but became an ordained minister in 1922 with the Disciples of Christ Church in Barbourville, Kentucky. He married a local woman, Sallie Stewart, but their marriage would only last five years.

Ford gained a reputation as an amazing speaker. He left the church to join the Swarthmore Chautauqua Association of Pennsylvania, going on the lecture circuit to talk about Spiritualism. After the war, the movement had seen a great surge in popularity and Ford became a speaker who was much in demand. He soon moved to New York and lectured to full houses at Carnegie Hall. He would slip into a trance state during his lectures, when he claimed to hear the voices of the dead, and he would deliver personal messages to people in the audience.

In 1924, a spirit named "Fletcher" announced that he would begin acting as Ford's contact with the next world. Fletcher had been a boyhood friend of Ford's and had been killed during the fighting in the war. In order for Fletcher to possess Ford, the medium would wrap a black silk handkerchief around his eyes, shutting out all light, and then would begin breathing deeply. Fletcher would assume control of Ford, relaying messages to the living. Ford claimed that he was never aware of Fletcher speaking through his vocal cords and never remembered anything that was said when the spirit took over his body.

With Fletcher's help, Ford's psychic ability became more impressive. He astounded audiences and even some his harshest critics. In the late 1920s, he formed the First Spiritualist Church of

After the death of her husband, Bess Houdini tried to communicate with his spirit for years. Arthur Ford was the only medium who offered possibly authentic messages from Houdini but whether or not he really reached his spirit remains controversial to this day.

New York and traveled all over the world, challenging his critics and delivering what many felt was convincing evidence that he truly could communicate with the dead.

In 1929, Ford conducted a sitting for Bess Houdini, the widow of the late magician, Harry Houdini. Houdini had died in 1926 and prior to his death, he and Bess had arranged a secret code that would prove to her that he could make contact with her from beyond the grave. The code was a variation of an old "mind-reading act" that the Houdinis had devised years before and had always kept secret. The initial contact was to be two words: "Rosabelle, believe." For years, mediums had tried to produce this information for Bess but none had been successful --- until Arthur Ford. Bess was so convinced that Ford had produced a communication from her husband that she signed a sworn statement to that fact. Later, under pressure from friends and critics, she wavered but she never officially denied her sworn statement.

In 1930, Ford suffered a terrible automobile accident that would change the course of his life and lead to the near destruction of his psychic ability. Ford was driving through North Carolina with his sister and another woman as passengers, when a truck swerved into his lane and struck Ford's car. The two women were killed and Ford was hospitalized with internal injuries, a broken jaw and shattered ribs. While he was in the hospital, Ford's doctor, who was interested in psychic abilities, discovered that Ford had out of body experiences while on morphine. To experiment, the doctor gave him repetitive doses of the drug, eventually causing him to become addicted. Ford's struggle to overcome his addiction to morphine turned him into an insomniac. In order to sleep, he drank, and soon became an alcoholic.

Ford was still at the height of his career during this time and he worked to keep his personal problems away from the public. His abilities were faltering, due to the alcohol, and after his death, it was learned that he may have cheated during some of his more important sessions.

Ford remarried in 1938 and his and his new wife, an English widow named Valerie McKeown, settled in Hollywood. Ford was happy but the alcohol was taking a serious toll on his career. He missed lectures, suffered from blackouts and often showed up drunk at public gatherings. His spirit guide, Fletcher, ridiculed Ford while the medium was under possession. He stated that he would go away but Ford refused to stop drinking. Soon, his psychic power, and Fletcher, disappeared. His wife divorced him and his health deteriorated. By 1949, he was hospitalized for depression and had suffered a physical breakdown.

It would be Alcoholics Anonymous that would help Ford get back on his feet. Except for occasional benders, he managed to control his drinking. However, he never gave it up completely and always kept a stash of liquor in every house he lived in. His health never really recovered. He suffered from angina, heart attacks and mild diabetes. His psychic ability slowly began to return and it was said that whenever Ford got sick, he managed to send out a psychic "signal" to his friends, who had the sudden urge to check on Ford's well-being.

In the 1950s, Fletcher finally returned and Ford was able to resume his work as a medium. When he was 71, he conducted the most famous séance of his life. The event took place on television and was performed for Bishop James Pike. Pike's son had committed suicide at the age of 20 in 1966 and the distraught bishop was anxious to make contact with him. The show was taped in September 1967 and Ford allowed Fletcher to take control over him before a national audience. He delivered information that Pike believed to be authentic and although the séance was hotly debated in the press, the bishop's faith in the information never wavered and he went on to write a bestselling book about the experience.

Ford spent the last years of his life in Miami and died in January 1971. He was cremated and his ashes scattered over the ocean. His final words had been: "God help me." Not surprisingly, this was not the last communication from Arthur Ford. Following his death, mediums around the world claimed to receive contact from him, adding another chapter to the mystery that was the life of Arthur Ford.

Even today, Spiritualists (or some modern-day offshoot of them) still practice communication through spirit possession. It is more commonly referred to today as "channeling." This form of mediumship occurs when a person allows him- or herself to be taken over by another personality while in a trance. Although not much different than what Arthur Ford was doing with his spirit guide, Fletcher, many mediums claim that the spirits they are communing with are not just those of the dead, but other, higher beings, as well. In recent times, it has been fashionable to channel "entities" who dispense their own brand of wisdom and self-help.

In America, channeling became especially popular in the 1970s when the channeled writings of the entity "Seth," speaking through Jane Roberts, became best-selling books. The story of Seth really began in 1963, when Roberts and her husband, Robert Butts, began experimenting with a Ouija Board as part of Roberts' research for a book on extra-sensory perception. They soon began receiving coherent messages from a male personality who eventually identified himself as "Seth." Soon after (like Pearl Curran), Roberts claimed that she was hearing the messages in her head and the board was abandoned.

For the next 21 years, until Roberts' death in 1984, she held regular sessions in which she went into a trance and purportedly channeled messages from Seth. Butts served as her secretary, taking down notes in his own private shorthand and recording some of the messages on tape. The communications from Seth were known collectively as the "Seth Material" and consisted of a variety of monologues on philosophical and spiritual topics. The material that came through up until 1969 was published in a book that was written by Roberts and included sections that came directly from Seth. In January 1970, the spirit began dictating its own books, which were channeled verbatim. They eventually grew into 10 separate volumes. Sessions were held to gather the material at regular intervals, usually two times each week.

Seth described himself as an "energy personality essence no longer focused in physical reality" and claimed that he was independent of Roberts' subconscious. His demeanor was notably different from that of Roberts', as reported by witnesses who included Robert Butts, friends, acquaintances and students. He was at times stern, jovial and frequently assumed an accent that no one was able to identify. Seth stated that he had completed his earthly reincarnations and he was now speaking from an adjacent plane of existence. His goal was to educate humans and impart the principles that he set forth in the materials that he was dictating through Roberts.

Interestingly, Roberts remained skeptical regarding her unplanned role as Seth's spokesperson. An author herself, she continued her own writings and produced a number of fiction and non-fiction titles under her own name. No one questioned the source and nature of Seth more than Roberts did. It has to be noted that Seth's and Jane Roberts' separate books showed very different writing styles and personalities. Roberts' style was very terse while Seth's was usually warm and friendly. Roberts' books were subjected to the normal editing process and Seth's books were published just as they were dictated, with only occasional corrections for grammar and punctuation.

The mystery of Seth was silenced in September 1984 when Jane Roberts died at the age of 55. What remained behind was two decades of material, some published, some not, and all recorded on lined paper in Robert Butts' block lettering. Boxes upon boxes of his original Seth notes reside permanently in the prestigious Yale Archives in New Haven, where volunteers endeavor to commit Seth's words to a comprehensive computer database.

Roberts' death may have silenced Seth but the mystery did not end with her passing. Was Roberts really possessed by the spirit of some invisible entity? Or, was the whole thing some sort of contrived, literary scam?

The readers must decide that for themselves. Seth often stated that his possession of Jane Roberts was accomplished by her ability to "bridge" the distance between two worlds. In her, he found a suitable vessel that he could fill to pass on his many centuries of wisdom.

However, Roberts always wondered whether or not "Seth" was merely a fragment of her own higher consciousness, perhaps something like a multiple personality. Seth never disagreed with these musings, refusing to solve the mystery of his existence and allowing everyone the freedom to make up their own minds.

The only other alternative was that Roberts faked Seth for two decades. To do this, Roberts, a modestly educated young woman from New York, would have had to have dictated hundreds of thousands of pages of complex, revolutionary material, mostly in front of an audience, speaking with a vocal resonance, dialect and accent distinctly different from her own. On top of this, she was also able to simultaneously produce a collection of fiction and nonfiction works, in a completely different style, under her own name.

Those who are unfamiliar with the Seth writings may assume that the last alternative answer is the best one but those who personally knew Roberts, and even those who knew her only through her writings and Seth's writings, would discount the "hoax" theory as the least viable explanation.

After Seth became a paranormal phenomenon, many imitations followed. Similar to the rush of popular interest when Spiritualism first emerged in the 19th century, scores of "channelers" soon went into business, some charging exorbitant fees for their sittings. Interest in this new fad died out by the end of the 1980s, although some of the more prominent practitioners have retained their followings to this day.

Where the Spirit Moves...

What do we make of all of this strangeness, these weird tales of possession and instances when spirits from outside of our realm have invaded the bodies of the living? Can there be some truth to such stories or are there merely the work of overactive imaginations? Can all of this be explained away by science, coincidence and fraud?

The reader will have to ponder such things for himself as we delve deeper into the darker recesses of the minds of two young girls who once lived in Watseka, Illinois.

II. Watseka

The city of Watseka, known then as South Middleport, came into existence in 1858 after a dispute arose regarding a railroad line. It was an inauspicious beginning for the town, which sprang up from the prairies of Iroquois County.

Iroquois Country is the only county in the United States with this particular name, a title that was originally given to a confederation of American Indian tribes. According to tradition, a band of these Indians were once murdered on the banks of the river, now known as the Iroquois, by a party of Illiniwek warriors. The name of the river and county was chosen in their honor.

Iroquois County lies about 80 miles south of Chicago and is bounded on the east by the state of Indiana. To the north is Kankakee County and on the west is the county of Ford. The southern boundary is marked by Vermillion County and another portion of Ford. When the first settlers came here, they found thousands of acres of forest and windswept prairie grass but the region had a long history before the first homesteaders arrived.

The territory within the confines of present-day Iroquois County was in dispute long before Illinois became a state. Under the charter of 1609, and supported by General George Roger Clark's request,

Virginia laid claim to all of the land north and west of the Ohio River and organized it as Illinois, named for the Illiniwek Indians. In 1784, Virginia surrendered her claims to the territory and turned the land over to the government of the United States. The vast domain became known as the Northwest Territory. The lands of Iroquois County underwent several changes during the time when

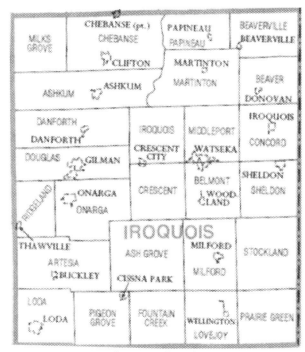

Iroquois County

it still fell within the borders of the Northwest Territory, first being a part of Knox County and then St. Clair, which was actually part of the Indiana Territory. Illinois was established as its own territory by an act of Congress in February 1803.

The region remained a part of St. Clair County until September 1812, when it joined with Edwards County. Later, the land was ceded to Crawford County, where it remained until Illinois was admitted into the Union in 1818. In 1819, the land was turned over to Clark County, until Edgar County was organized in 1823. After that, it was given to Vermillion County when it was organized in 1826 and then, finally, Iroquois became its own county on February 26, 1833.

The new county of Iroquois embraced all of the territory from what is now the north line of Vermillion County to the south line of Cook County. It would lose sections of land in the years to come when Will County was created in 1836, extending south to the Kankakee River. The river, except for a short distance at the northwest corner of the county, became the northern boundary of Iroquois County. In 1853, Kankakee County was created from territory that was taken from both Will and Iroquois Counties. From this point, Iroquois was limited to its present boundaries.

In 1835, the town of Montgomery offered the county 20 acres of land on which to locate a permanent county seat. The land was located just east of Montgomery and was platted as a town site in 1836 under the name of Iroquois. The county accepted the offer and the county seat was established in Iroquois. Then, for some reason, nothing ever happened. No buildings were erected and so the county was forced to rent offices and a courtroom in Montgomery. Everyone just seemed to wait around for something to happen in Iroquois and since nothing ever did, the town site was abandoned.

There was a general dissatisfaction about having the county offices in Montgomery because most agreed that it was too far from the center of the county. In 1838, an act was obtained from the Illinois legislature to relocate the county seat. The town of Middleport offered the county land on which the county seat could be located and the offer was accepted. The new county seat was located in Middleport in 1839.

The first county building to be erected was the jail. It was rough-hewn from logs and cost the county $159 to build. In 1843, officials decided to build a two-story brick courthouse. The lower level was to be used as a courtroom, with offices for county officials on the second floor. To defray the cost of the new structure, the sum of $1,506 was appropriated from county funds. To this was added the sale of the remaining town lots that the city of Montgomery had donated when the county seat was located there.

To raise the rest of the money, the county planned to sell off some land that it owned along the Salt Fork River west of Danville. The land had what should have been a profitable salt spring on it but it had never been developed. Plans had been in the works to turn the spring into a commercial enterprise, funds from which were going to build bridges over the Vermillion and Iroquois rivers, but development never got off the ground. Iroquois County decided to sell off its share of the land and sent a representative to Danville to dispose of it. Unfortunately, no one wanted it. The best offer that he could obtain was to trade the land for a horse. The trade was made and the horse was taken to Chicago and sold. The records don't state just how much money the sale of the horse added to the courthouse fund. Nevertheless, the building was completed in 1847.

The death knell for Middleport – and the beginnings of Watseka – came in 1858. In that year, the Peoria and Oquawka Railroad began building its line east from Peoria to the Indiana state line. The route was surveyed through Middleport, which should have been great news to residents and business owners, but instead, a dispute arose that involved the donation of town land for a depot. The deal stalled and the railroad owners were stuck waiting for the people of Middleport to solve their problems.

Meanwhile, a group of local men who owned land to the south of Middleport decided to make an offer to the railroad that would allow the line to bypass the town altogether. The offer was accepted and the route ran to the south, creating a controversy that simmered for years. A new town, first called South Middleport, came into existence and slowly began to prosper. Thanks to the railroad, businesses and homes began to spring up in South Middleport and in 1865, the name of the town was changed to Watseka. When the new town was incorporated, it swallowed Middleport and the original town ceased to exist as a separate community.

The old courthouse was abandoned and a new one was built in Watseka. On October 16, 1866, around 2 a.m., the new courthouse caught fire and many of the country records were destroyed. It was believed that the fire was set by citizens of Middleport disgruntled over the loss of their town and the removal of the courthouse to Watseka. It would be many years before the grievances over the railroad deal would be forgiven in Watseka. There would be many who would hold the landowners who made the deal to convince the railroad to bypass the town responsible for the problems that some Middleport business owners came to face with the loss of commerce.

One of these landowners was a prominent businessman named Asa Berry Roff, who was dealing with the illness of his beloved daughter, a young woman named Mary.

Asa Roff was born in Morris County, New Jersey, on September 13, 1818. His family moved to New York when he was three years old, where his father died a few years later. Roff's mother returned to New Jersey with her other children but, for reasons unknown, left Asa to be raised by his uncle. Roff had a miserable childhood under the strict discipline of his uncle, who apprenticed him to a shoemaker when he was 13. Roff spent the next six years working off the contract that his uncle had obtained for his work. He rarely saw any of the money that he made. When he turned 19, he started off on his own, traveling first to Albany, New York, then on to Michigan and finally, to Indiana. He worked for a time in Logansport and then he and his brother traveled downriver in canoes to Independence, where he went to work for a shoemaker.

On January 3, 1841, Roff married a local young woman named

Asa Roff, later in his life, long after the events involving his daughter and Lurancy Vennum

Dorothy Ann Fenton, who was seven years younger than her new husband. The couple lived in Warren County, Indiana until the fall of 1847, when they packed up and came to Iroquois County. Over the course of their lives, Asa and Dorothy had 10 children: William, who died at the age of 2; George, who died in infancy; Minerva, who was born in 1844; Frances who died in 1850 at the age of 5; Joseph, who lived from 1856 to 1924; Fenton; Gaylord, who lived only one year; Frank; Charles, who died as a young man in 1885; and Mary, who died in 1865 at the age of 18.

In September 1847, the Roffs came to Illinois and settled in Middleport, which was then the county seat. Roff took over a harness shop in town and also began selling shoes. He quickly made a name for himself as an astute businessman and in 1849, was appointed the town's postmaster. He was soon elected to the office of justice of the peace and in 1854, was named sheriff and became a tax collector for Iroquois County for two years.

Although Roff had left school with little formal education, he began to study law on his own and in 1856, was admitted to the Illinois bar association. A short time later, he formed a partnership with Robert Doyle, a young attorney who had just come to town. They remained partners for the next nine years, dealing with both criminal cases and real estate.

It would be Roff's knowledge of real estate law that would serve him well in 1858 when the Peoria and Oquawka Railroad came to Middleport looking for land to build their new line. After a dispute started in town over the depot location, Roff and several other men offered land that they owned south of town as an alternative to the Middleport route. Roff had purchased an interest in a sawmill there in 1852 and while he only manufactured lumber for about 18 months, he maintained ownership of the land.

The railroad accepted their offer and South Middleport – soon to be known as Watseka – was born.

Over the course of the next years, the lives of the Roff family were filled with spectacular highs and lows. In 1863, when the first post

Walnut Street in Watseka on the late 1800s

office was established in Watseka, Roff was appointed as the postmaster, a position that he maintained until 1866. The year 1865 saw the final deterioration and death of Mary Roff. In 1868, Roff built the first brick house in Watseka, which is still located on North Fifth Street today. His daughter, Minerva, and her husband, Henry Alter, took over the ownership of the original Roff house in town, which was one of the first frame houses in Watseka.

Once again, however, as the Roff family found peace and security, it was torn away from them. Financial troubles came in 1873 and over the course of the next two years, Roff saw business failures and real estate foreclosures. He had borrowed more than $20,000 against various properties that he owned but the bank called in his notes and the loans were made worthless.

During this time of trouble, the Roffs turned to the Spiritualist movement. There is no indication as to what may have attracted them to Spiritualism but perhaps the death of a number of their children, especially Mary, who had died just a few years before, had given them a need to try and communicate with the other side. Whatever the reason behind their decision, Asa and Dorothy Ann embraced the movement wholeheartedly and became well known for their beliefs. They started a Spiritualist society in Watseka and held many meetings at their home on Fifth Street.

Around this same time, Roff was elected to the position of justice of the peace again and his financial and personal problems of recent years seemed to be fading into the past.

Then came the strange events of 1878 --- and life for the Roff family would never be the same again.

III. The Possessed

The town of Watseka, which boasted about 1,500 souls in the late 1870s, was little more than a sleepy farming community at the time that the Watseka Wonder left an indelible mark on the history of the city. Aside from the courthouse fire and the lingering resentment over the disappearance of the town of Middleport, little out of the ordinary ever occurred here.

The boredom of small town life was shattered forever on July 11, 1877.

It was on this day that a 13-year-old girl named Lurancy Vennum first fell into a mysterious, catatonic trance during which she claimed that she was able to speak to angels and the spirits of the dead. The strange spells would often occur many times each day and some of them would last for hours. During the trances, Lurancy would speak in different voices and tell of places far away that she had no real knowledge about. When she woke up, she wouldn't remember anything that she said or did while she was under the influence of these spells. Word quickly spread around town that odd things were happening at the home of Thomas and Lurinda Vennum and soon the news began to spread out of town, to Chicago and around the state. Soon, many visitors began to arrive in Watseka, all hoping to see the young girl.

The news of these strange trances gained much attention within the Spiritualist community for many believed that Lurancy was manifesting mediumistic abilities during her trances. Soon, Spiritualists from all over Illinois, and from around the country, came to Watseka to see if the stories were true.

Lurancy Vennum

The Vennum family was not interested in mediums and Spiritualists, however. They were only concerned with the health and welfare of their daughter and they took her to one physician after another in hopes that someone would be able to help her. The doctors could find nothing physically wrong with Lurancy and they eventually diagnosed her as being mentally ill. It was recommended that she be sent to the state insane asylum in Peoria. Heartbroken, the Vennums felt they had no other choice and after the holiday season of 1877, they began to make arrangements to have their daughter committed. They knew there was little chance that Lurancy would ever come home again.

But before Lurancy could be sent away, in January 1878, a man named Asa Roff arrived at the home of the Vennum family. He explained to them that his own daughter, Mary, had been afflicted with the same condition that Lurancy was suffering from. He begged the Vennums not to send Lurancy to the asylum. He had mistakenly sent his own daughter away years before and she had later died. Despite her death, though, he was convinced that his daughter's spirit still existed. And little did he know it would soon become apparent to many that his daughter's spirit was now inside of the body of Lurancy Vennum.

This was the beginning of a series of strange and fantastic events that rocked the little town of Watseka and created a mystery that remains unsolved to this day. To understand the events, we must first start at the beginning of the story and try to put together the pieces of the puzzle that has fascinated researchers, historians and the general public for more than a century.

Mary Roff

Asa Roff's daughter Mary was born on October 8, 1846 in Warren County, Indiana, a little less than a year before the Roff family came to Illinois and settled in Middleport. Starting at the age of six months, Mary began to suffer from strange seizures, which over the course of her life gradually increased in violence. When the attacks began, she was a tiny infant and her condition paralyzed the Roffs with fear, especially after the earlier deaths of two of their children, William and George. Strangely, though, even though Mary lay in a coma-like state for several days, she soon recovered and, within few weeks, seemed perfectly fine.

Unfortunately, her periods of good health would not last. A few weeks later, another spell seized her. Her pupils would dilate and she would become very stiff and her muscles would twitch uncontrollably for a short time. The seizure would then be followed by a period of eerie calm that could last for minutes, hours or even days. Once it came to an end, she would behave normally, as if no illness afflicted her --- at least until she suffered from another spate of puzzling illness. The spells came every three to five weeks and as she grew older, they became more violent and more prolonged.

As Mary grew older, and the seizures became more horrifying, she also began to complain of mysterious voices that she heard in her head. The voices, she said, came from nowhere and told her to do things that she knew she shouldn't. Even her periods of good health seemed to be marked by a depression and despondency that should not have been present in a beautiful young girl who was so dearly loved by her parents and her sister Minerva. Mary could often be found sitting in the parlor of their home, playing mournful music and singing sad songs. A feeling of doom seemed to linger about her, as if she knew terrible events were coming.

By the time Mary was 15, her health had grown worse. The Roffs had taken her to see doctors all over the region, including Dr. Jesse Bennett and

Mary Roff

Dr. Franklin Blades of Watseka, and several prominent physicians in Chicago, including Dr. N.S. Davis. Davis was a professor at the Northwestern University Medical School and a well-known homeopathic physician. He not only helped to charter a homeopathic medical college in Chicago but also pressed for reforms for the city's health. He led the campaign in 1862 for the city to hire a health officer and to start a citywide board of health. Asa Roff spared no expense in trying to get treatment for Mary, seeking out the best Illinois medical men of the time, but it was all to no avail. No one could discover what was wrong with her. It eventually was suggested that she be sent to a sanitarium run by a Dr. Nevins in Peoria for treatment.

The sanitarium was similar to many that dotted the American landscape during the 1850s and 1860s. It was known simply as a "water cure," or hydropathic institution, and it offered an alternative to the usual practice of medicine by promising a healthier life through simple, natural drug-free means. It was based on the use of

(Left) A typical water cure hospital of the middle 1800s

(Below) Water Cures became so popular that a print journal was devoted to them

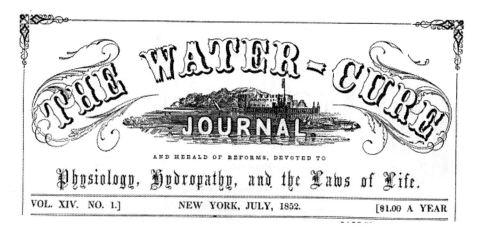

THE WATER-CURE JOURNAL.

AND HERALD OF REFORMS, DEVOTED TO

Physiology, Hydropathy, and the Laws of Life.

VOL. XIV. NO. 1.]   NEW YORK, JULY, 1852.   [$1.00 A YEAR

pure, soft, mineral-free water in various forms of baths, wet wraps and internal cleansing. Treatment also included other "natural" treatments like exercise, fresh air, and a vegetarian diet that was rich in fruits and grains. The use of alcohol and tobacco was strictly prohibited and ladies who came to the clinic were encouraged to wear loose-fitting clothing.

By this time, Mary's doctors had come to believe that her spells and seizures were caused by some sort of "female ailment" and so a water cure seemed to be the prefect answer. Water cure sanitariums

The Possessed -- Page 64

held a special appeal for women. Most members of the medical community at this time treated women's issues, like menstruation, childbirth and menopause as unnatural occurrences to be dealt with aggressively but the water cure advocates treated them as natural events that they believed could be eased by exercise, diet, calmness and baths. In addition, there were usually female doctors on staff to attend to the ladies since hydropathic medical schools were among the only places that women who wanted to study medicine found acceptance.

Patients like Mary who came for a water cure were instructed to bring with them certain items that were needed for treatment: two large wool blankets, three comforters, two coarse cotton sheets, one coarse linen sheet, six towels and pieces of cotton for bandages. During the course of water treatments, Mary was immersed naked into a tub of water and then placed into a tub of very hot water. She would also receive a cold water douche and wet sheets were wrapped tightly around her body to restrict her circulation, followed by vigorous rubbing to restore her circulation to normal. She would later go for a strenuous walk and then return to her room for a nap, where she would be wrapped with several blankets and comforters, leaving only her face exposed.

There were few illnesses that could not be "treated" by a water cure, which purported to cure colds, weak constitutions, fevers, poor circulation, gout, alcoholism and even seizures and insanity. And while the treatment may seem harsh, or even shocking, it was preferable to most general medicine of the day, which relied heavily on purgatives, enemas, laxatives and bloodletting for treating illnesses. The water cure was not only gentler but could actually be effective.

Mary remained at Dr. Nevins' sanitarium for 18 months, during which time she improved and relapsed several times. Her weird seizures continued, frightening the other patients, until finally, in the late spring of 1864, she markedly improved and the doctor was able to send her home to Watseka. He truly believed that she had been

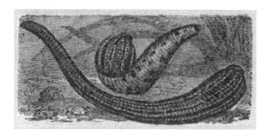

(Above) A Scientific drawing of Medical Leeches

(Right) An 1840 Staffordshire pedestal-shaped leeches jar. Many doctors who commonly used leeches would store the creatures in their office in jars like this one.

cured and Mary finally seemed to be well --- at least for a time.

As summer approached, Mary began to complain of sharp, stabbing pains in her head. She called it a "lump of pain" and the only way that she seemed to be able to alleviate the discomfort was by bleeding herself. She developed an obsession with blood and began stabbing herself with pins and cutting herself with a straight razor. A local doctor and druggist, F. Conrad Secrest was called in he began applying leeches to Mary.

Bloodletting was a part of medical practice that dated back to ancient times and became particularly popular in America during the middle part of the 1800s. It was believed that by draining the blood, balance could be restored to the body. It was accomplished in two ways – either by cutting into a vein and letting blood escape, or by applying leeches, which took blood at a slow, predictable rate and then fell off when full.

Leeches were used for bloodletting in ancient Greece and Rome and they continued to be a part of European medical practice

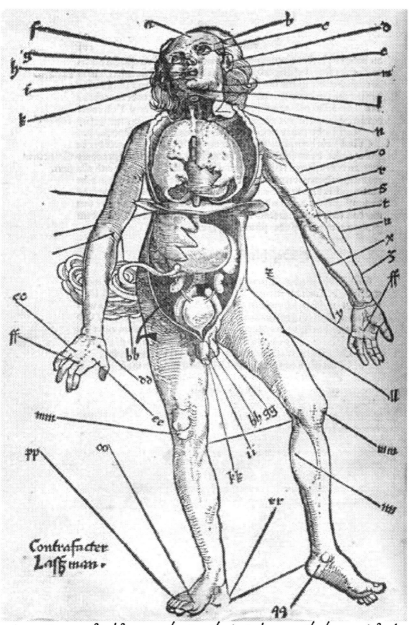

Contrafacter
Laßman.

An antique medical diagram showing the best places on the human body for
blood-letting and the application of leeches

throughout the ages. The word "leech" even comes from an Old English word for physician. The practice remained popular for years and with the dawn of science, leeches became even more widely used. In the first half of the 19th century, scientific journals were full of articles extolling their virtues and trade in medicinal leeches became a major industry.

The use of leeches was often quite gruesome. They could be applied almost anywhere, including the gums, lips, nose, fingers, breasts, and even "the mouth of the womb." They were most commonly applied to the temples and prolonged use would leave the patient with small x-shaped scars where the leeches had fed. Dozens of leeches could be applied at a time. When they were full, they were stored in special jars until they were ready to be used again. Sometimes, a patient would be bled continuously for days at a time.

For some reason, Dr. Secrest left a supply of leeches at the Roff home and Mary would apply them to herself whenever she felt anxious or complained of a headache. She applied them to her temples and it was said that she treated them like pets. A bleeding session, which could last for 45 minutes or so, usually alleviated whatever pain she was feeling.

But on some days, the small amount of blood drawn by a leech or a straight pin was not enough. On Saturday morning, July 16, 1864, Mary took a knife and slipped outside to a hiding place in the backyard. She began cutting her arm and lost so much blood that she fainted. She was found several hours later and was carried into the house. It was some time before she stirred but when she did, she began to thrash violently about and scream as though she were being tortured. Her convulsions and screams continued almost non-stop for the next five days and nights. The Roffs required the almost constant services of five strong men to hold her down on the bed. Mary bucked and kicked, punched and thrashed throughout the night and into the daylight hours. No one could explain the brutal force being manifested by this young girl.

Finally, on the fifth day, the ravings ceased and Mary's demeanor became strangely serene. She regained consciousness and appeared to be quite normal, expect for one thing – she claimed not to recognize anyone in her family, nor her doctors, friends or neighbors. The house was filled with well-meaning acquaintances, as well as friends of Asa Roff, but Mary did not appear to know any of them. In addition to this peculiar development, Mary was able to speak of places where she had never been, often with uncanny accuracy. In addition, she was reportedly able to predict future events and she knew things about people that she should have had no way of knowing.

She also began to manifest a very strange, clairvoyant ability that allowed her to read and do anything else that she normally did in the course of her daily life, all while wearing a blindfold. Her eyes covered by a heavy blindfold, Mary would dress, stand before the mirror, open and search drawers, puck up various items and do whatever she customarily did.

The Roffs and their friends were amazed by this startling new ability and Mary was frequently put to the test by various ministers, newspaper reporters and "all of the prominent citizens of Watseka at that time."

During one of the tests, Mary was handed a thick medical encyclopedia and

Blindfold tests, such as those carried out on Mary Roff, were often used by Spiritualists to check for clairvoyant abilities.

asked to find a listing for "blood." She turned to the index, while blindfolded, traced her fingers along the thousands of entries, pointed to the word "blood" and then opened the book to the page that was indicated and managed to read the entry. On another occasion, she took a box of letters that had been sent to her by friends and sat down, with a blindfold on, and read them aloud for the doctors, ministers and businessmen who were present. When The Reverend J.H. Rhea, newspaper editor A.G. Smith, Asa Roff and several others arranged some of their own letters with those that had been written to Mary, she proceeded to pull out these letters and examine them. If any were turned wrong-side up, she would reverse them, read aloud the addresses that were written on them and violently toss aside any letter that was not her own.

No one could explain how she was able to do these things. They were as mysterious as the spells that had been troubling her since she was an infant. Most of the physicians who treated Mary referred to her condition as catalepsy, a popular diagnosis of the nineteenth century.

Catalepsy is a condition that is characterized by rigid muscles and limbs, a loss of muscle control and a slowing down of bodily functions, like breathing. For this reason, many sufferers were mistakenly declared dead and this allegedly led to many premature burials in years past. In modern times, it has been learned that catalepsy does not appear of its own accord and instead, manifests as one of many symptom caused by disorders that have physical causes, ranging from Parkinson's disease to epilepsy. In some cases, isolated cataleptic instances can also be precipitated by extreme emotional shock, but this is rare.

Most medical professionals in years past, especially those in the time of Mary Roff, believed that catalepsy was caused by a mental disorder. For this reason, they suspected that Mary was slipping into a cataleptic trance whenever she was by seized by one of her spells. However, this diagnosis did not explain how she obtained knowledge that she should not have had, was able to foresee future events, and

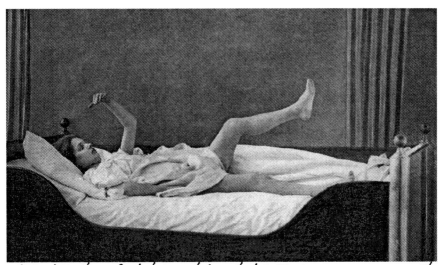

(Above) In this medical photograph from the late 1800s, a young woman with catalepsy is shown. The disease afflicted her left arm and leg, which would be seized and stiff for as long as an hour before slowly relaxing.

could use clairvoyant powers to see and read through a blindfold. All of these "symptoms" remained unexplained.

For just this reason, some of the ministers who were called to the Roff home to examine Mary and witness her strange feats called her powers "a mystery of God's providence." They could find no explanation for how she was accomplishing such things and merely left the answers to the mysteries of divine intervention.

Perhaps the most perplexed by what was occurring were the newspaper editors and writers who came to visit the Roffs. These men could not look toward medical science for answers and their own cynicism kept them from simply leaving the mystery in the hands of God. They knew that Mary's abilities, and her illness, were the result of some unaccountable phenomenon, but just what that was, they were unprepared to say.

A.G. Smith, the editor of the *Iroquois County Republican* at the time of Mary Roff's death and the editor of the *Danville Times* during

Lurancy Vennum's possession, later wrote about Mary:

Now, as to Mary Roff, it was our fortune to know the sweet girl, who was herself a cataleptic, and who died twelve years ago. Disease dethroned her reason and maddened her brain until she sought her own and other's lives, and the modest young lady was transformed into a screaming maniac. She had periods of exemption from raving, and thus her aberrant mind conceived fancies of the queerest hue, creating the most impossible beings for associates, and conversing with them, she maintained her own side of the conversation in a usual tone of voice, while imagination supplied her created associates with language and intelligence. When in this condition, her father and mother asserted the discovery that Mary could read a book with its lid closed, and they desired us to test the correctness of what they claimed. We therefore took from our side pocket a letter enclosed in an envelope, and holding it before he bandaged eyes, said to her. "Mary, read the signature to that letter." Immediately, the proper name was pronounced.

Mary remained in what was referred to as her "clairvoyant state" for three or four days, still not recognizing anyone, and then finally, seemed to regain her wits and began acting like herself again. She was once again conscious of those around her, recognized her family and friends and lost the ability to psychically "see" through a blindfold. Unfortunately, her return to what passed for normalcy meant the loss of the serene calmness that had accompanied her clairvoyant abilities and the return of her violent seizures.

The episodes came over and over again, causing Mary great pain and distress, and she would sometimes remain unconscious and rigid on the floor, or in her bed, for hours or days at a time. She never moved except when she was first seized by a spell, which often elicited horrifying screams, and when she came out of one. Her return to consciousness was often accompanied by the violent thrashing about that sometimes required several men to hold her down.

After coming out of her seizures, Mary began to speak of what she saw when she was unconscious. Angels and spirits spoke to her and traveled with her as she looked over places that she had never before visited. In time, she began to claim that these beings accompanied her back from "the other side" and were present in the Roff house. When Mary spoke with them, her friends and family saw nothing and never heard the other side of the conversations that she claimed to be having with the spirits.

Mary's condition worsened and finally, feeling they had no other choice, Asa and Dorothy Ann Roff accepted the advice that they had been given by several of Mary's doctors: they would place the girl in an insane asylum. All of the other possible avenues had been exhausted. No doctor could find a cure for her problem and, in fact, none of them could even agree on what the problem actually was. Despite the eerie abilities that Mary manifested for a time, there seemed to be no explanation for what was wrong with her other than that she was mentally ill.

Arrangements were made to send her away and all of this was carried out with the Roffs never realizing that Mary would not return home alive.

The Insane Asylum

Placing Mary in an insane asylum was not a step that the Roffs took lightly. They had done everything that they could think of to find a cure for Mary's condition. They had allowed her to stay at Dr. Nevins' water cure facility, at great expense, for nearly 18 months and had spent a small fortune on doctors, treatments and possible solutions. All of it had been to no avail and they had little choice but to consider the idea that whatever was wrong with Mary was all in her mind.

Tragically, though, sending her to the asylum offered no real chance for a cure. An insane asylum of the 1860s was not a place that was designed to treat the mentally ill. It was actually a place where

Popular Mode of Curing Insanity!

Lizzie Bonner punishing Miss Hodson, on suspicion of taking her key.

A popular illustration dramatizing the conditions of insane asylums in the middle and late 1800s.

these so afflicted were warehoused and kept away from mainstream society in the same way that prisons were used to house criminals. Conditions were often extremely poor and treatment was not yet an option. Many asylums were barely fit for human habitation. They were filthy places of confinement where patients were often left in straitjackets, locked in restraints or even placed in cages if they were especially disturbed. Many of the inmates spent every day in shackles and chains.

This would have been the type of asylum that Mary Roff would have been sent to 1865. According to records, she was indeed sent to an asylum, and later died there, but the question remains as to where this asylum may have been located. Most versions of the Watseka Wonder case state that the Roffs had Mary committed at the State

Insane Asylum in Peoria but this is a problem because the asylum in Peoria did not exist at that time. In fact, it would not even be constructed until 1885. Even then, it would remain open for a few years before being torn down and rebuilt in 1902.

So, if Mary Roff was not committed to the asylum in Peoria, then where was she sent? At the time, the only state insane asylum in Illinois was located in Jacksonville. This asylum, known as the Illinois State Hospital for the Insane, came about in 1847 due to an act of the legislature and the efforts of Dorothea L. Dix, a social reformer and advocate for the insane and the incarcerated. Construction was started on the asylum in 1848 and it opened in 1851. It would be more than four years after Mary's death that a second hospital was opened in Cook County, followed by the Elgin Hospital in 1872; Anna State Hospital in 1875; the Kankakee Hospital in 1879; the Chester State Hospital in 1891; and finally, the Peoria (or Bartonville) Asylum in 1902.

Was Mary sent to the hospital in Jacksonville? If she was, then why has it always been stated that she was sent to Peoria – to a hospital that did not even exist at the time?

It's possible that some confusion came to the story for two different reasons. It may be that some writers confused the two hospitals where Mary spent time before her death. At one point, she was in Peoria, staying at Dr. Nevins' Water Cure, but was sent back home before she was finally committed to the asylum. It's possible that these two stays, in different sanitariums, were accidentally combined into one. It's also possible that, in the early 1900s, writers who looked into the case (this was a popular time for re-examination, as we will see later) simply noted that Mary was committed to the "state insane asylum." The new hospital in Peoria was commonly described as this for many years and perhaps the writers assumed that the hospital was located in Peoria.

To be accurate, though, if Mary Roff was sent to the state insane asylum in 1865, then she would have had to have been sent to the asylum in Jacksonville. Dr. Nevins' Water Cure was not an asylum

The Jacksonville State Hospital in the 1860s. At the time of Mary Roff's incarceration and death, it was the only state hospital in Illinois

and was not a place where mentally ill patients were commonly treated. There is no record of a private insane asylum in Peoria at that time and in those days, such things really did not exist. She was placed, the records say, "in the insane asylum," so that would have been in Jacksonville at the Illinois State Hospital for the Insane.

Conditions at the state asylum were similar to conditions that were being reported around the country at that time and it's likely that Mary found her stay at such a place to be a terrifying ordeal. Her physical health began to fail as she continued to endure her seizures and was subjected to the grim conditions of the hospital.

Asa and Dorothy Roff made as many trips to see their daughter as possible. Visiting time was restricted by hospital officials but the Roffs were able to come on successive days if they stayed somewhere locally. On July 5, 1865, they were on the third day of a visit to the hospital when Mary died. She had been able to sit down with them for breakfast but soon after had returned to her room for a nap. She drifted off to sleep but a few minutes later, she began to let out some familiar screams. They were the same bloodcurdling cries that came before Mary was gripped by one of her spells. Her parents were summoned, in hopes that they might be able to calm Mary down, but by the time they arrived at her room, the girl had gone quiet.

Mary's seizure had not passed. She had died. At the age of 18, Mary Roff had been taken from this world, leaving a scar on her parent's hearts that was so deep that they turned to the Spiritualist movement to make sense of what had happened to her.

At the time of Mary Roff's death, Lurancy Vennum was a little more than one year old. In just over a decade, though, the two girls' lives would be forever connected in a case that still remains one of the strangest, and most authentic, cases of spirit possession ever recorded.

Lurancy Vennum

Mary Lurancy Vennum, or 'Rancy as she was usually called, was born on April 16, 1864, in Milford, a small community that was located about seven miles south of Watseka. After living in Iowa for a year, the Vennums returned to Milford and a few years later, when Lurancy, was about seven, moved to Watseka. This was long after Mary Roff's brief moments of notoriety in town and her tragic death. The Vennum family knew nothing of the girl, her strange illness or anything about the Roff family at all. The only acquaintance between the two families came during one brief call that Mrs. Roff made on Mrs. Vennum after they moved to Watseka in 1871. Mr. Roff and Mr. Vennum were on formal speaking terms but had never had any reason to make the acquaintance of the other. The families lived on extreme opposite sides of the city.

Lurancy was the daughter of Thomas Jefferson Vennum, who had been born in Washington County, Pennsylvania, in 1832. He had come to Illinois with his family when he was still a child and a number of Vennums were some of the first settlers of Iroquois County. His wife, Lurinda J. Smith, was born in Indiana in 1837 and they were married in Fayette County, Iowa in 1855. He had been a farmer all of his life but his wife had asked him to move the family into town after he received a small inheritance from the sale of a farm in Iowa. Vennum was well liked in the community when his family's trouble began in July 1877.

Lurancy had never been a sickly girl, nor an especially imaginative one. For both reasons, her family was surprised when the strange events began. Save for a bout with measles in 1873, she had never been seriously ill and until 1877, she had never made up stories or told fanciful tales about much of anything at all. However, in the early days of July, she began speaking of mysterious voices that came to her in the night.

According to her story, they had roused her from her sleep. She stated: "There were persons in my room last night, and they called 'Rancy, Rancy...' and I felt their breath upon my face." She seemed to be frightened and disturbed by what had occurred and was convinced that she had not dreamed it. Her parents had never known her to lie but, not believing in such things, were not inclined to give credence to her story. They merely assumed that their daughter had experienced a very vivid nightmare, one so real that she believed that she was awake when it happened.

The following night, though, the same thing happened again. Lurancy refused to stay in her room. She rose in the dead of night and nervously paced the parlor, too frightened to return to her second-floor bedroom. She told her mother that each time she tried to sleep, the presences would return, whispering her name. Finally, Lurinda took Lurancy back to her room and they lay down together on the bed. She wrapped her arms around her daughter and coaxed her back to sleep. The rest of the night passed without incident.

But on July 11, 1877, the possession truly began.

On that otherwise ordinary morning, Lurancy got out of bed feeling very dizzy and nauseated. She complained to her mother about feeling sick but went about her household chores as usual. Around six o'clock that evening, after the day's heat had begun to fade, Lurinda asked Lurancy to help her start supper. Lurancy had been sewing a carpet that afternoon and she put aside her things and rose to come into the kitchen.

Suddenly, she spoke: "Ma, I feel bad. I feel so queer." She grabbed at her left breast with her hand, then collapsed to the floor. She was so quiet that she seemed to be dead and every muscle in her body had gone rigid and cold.

She stayed in a deep, catatonic sleep for the next five hours but when she woke up, she said she felt fine. But this was just the beginning. The following day, Lurancy again slipped into a trance-like sleep but this time was different. This time, as she lay perfectly still, she began to speak out loud, talking of visions and spirits and carrying on conversations with people that no one else could see. She told her family that she was in heaven and that she could see and hear spirits. She described them and called some of them by name. Among them was her brother, who she affectionately called "Bertie." He had died in when Lurancy was only three years old.

In the days and weeks that followed, Lurancy's spells came more and more frequently and they sometimes lasted for more than eight hours at a time. While she was in her trance state, she continued to speak about her visions, which were sometimes terrifying. She began to see more and more spirits, including those who had terrorized her at night in her bedroom. So many of them were unfamiliar and strange to her and she would cry out while in the midst of her spells. At times, Lurancy reportedly spoke in other languages, or at least spouted nonsense words that no one could understand. She lapsed into lengthy trances that would sometimes last for hours each day. When she awoke, she would remember nothing of what had happened during the trance and was always ignorant of her weird ramblings.

The frightening trances lasted throughout the summer months but at some point in September 1877, they stopped. Lurancy seemed to be herself again and although her mother watched her cautiously for several weeks, the bizarre illness seemed to be gone. Gradually, life in the Vennum household began to return to normal.

But these times of normalcy were not destined to last.

On November 27, 1877, Lurancy began to complain of a violent

The Thomas Vennum house as it looks today. It was here that Lurancy is believed to have become possessed by the spirit of Mary Roff

pain in her stomach. The pain remained a dull, throbbing ache but several times each day, it became excruciating. The sharp, stabbing pain would always come on quite suddenly, making Lurancy scream and moan in torment. She would fall to the floor, her teeth grinding in agony, as the pain ripped through her body. It was later reported: "In these painful paroxysms, she would double herself back until her head and feet actually touched."

These horrendous episodes went on for about two weeks, only coming to an end on December 11, when Lurancy slipped once more into one of the dreaded trances that her parents thought had gone away. She was seized by one of these spells and slowly sank to the floor, completely unconscious. Her body rigidly remained in the same position for the next several hours but when she awakened, the abdominal pains were gone.

Unfortunately, though, the spells had returned. For the next several weeks, the trances came over her and lasted for two hours, three hours or even as long as eight hours. They occurred as many as 12 times each day, sending Lurancy into a place where she once again began to speak with the spirits that she saw there. She called them "angels" and held long eerie conversations with them, of which she would remember nothing when she finally regained consciousness.

Shortly after the trances had begun, Lurancy was placed under the care of Dr. L.N. Pittwood, who, although one of the city's best-known medical practitioners, could find nothing physically wrong with her. The family turned to Dr. Jewett for answers after the stomach pains and new spells, but he was also at a loss as to what was causing the illness. Many of the friends and family members of the Vennums believed that Lurancy had gone insane and the family's minister, The Reverend B.M. Baker from the Methodist Church, went as far as to contact the state asylum in Jacksonville to see if the girl could be admitted there. It was the general feeling among those whose counsel the Vennums valued, that the girl should be institutionalized.

Stories and rumors about Lurancy and her visions began to circulate in Watseka. People were talking about the weird happenings and the local newspaper printed stories about them. No one followed the case more closely than Asa Roff did. During his own daughter's illness, she had also claimed to communicate with spirits and she fell into long, sometimes violent, trances. He became convinced that Lurancy Vennum was suffering with the same affliction that Mary had. In spite of this, Roff said nothing until the Vennum family had exhausted every known cure for Lurancy and it appeared that she was going to be sent away to the asylum. At this point, he became determined to try and help.

Asa Roff called on the Vennum family in late January 1878. The family was naturally skeptical of the reason for his visit. Roff had little more than a casual acquaintance with Thomas Vennum but he explained that he had become interested in Lurancy's case after hearing the rumors that were going on in town. Lurancy claimed to have had contact with the spirits of the dead, the possibility of which, being a devout Spiritualist, he did not doubt in the slightest. However, his real interest was concerning her illness. He himself had once had a daughter, Mary, who had suffered from an identical condition and who had also given incontrovertible evidence of supernatural powers in the form of clairvoyance. In her time, Mary had also been regarded as insane, although now, years later, Roff was convinced that she had been of sound mind but had been the victim of a "spirit infestation." He believed that the same could be said of Lurancy and he begged the Vennums not to send their daughter to an asylum.

He believed there was a way to help the girl and he convinced the Vennums to allow him to call in one more physician. If there was nothing that this man could do, then they could take whatever steps they believed were necessary to try and help Lurancy.

With some reluctance, the Vennums agreed to his plea and although they didn't know it at the time, their lives would never be the same again.

Dr. Stevens Arrives

Roff returned to the Vennum house in the company of Dr. E. Winchester Stevens on January 31. Dr. Stevens was a physician from Janesville, Wisconsin, who, like Roff, was a devout Spiritualist. He was curious about the case, having visited Watseka a few times and heard about it during the preceding fall, and wanted to offer whatever help he could to the beleaguered family. His interest had been piqued by the medical aspects of the case and by the possibility that Lurancy might be "spirit infested," as he had come to believe that his friend's daughter, Mary Roff, had been.

Stevens and Roff were considering the idea that Lurancy was a sort of vessel through which the dead were communicating. Roff only wished that he had seen the same evidence in his own daughter years before. He believed that if Mary had actually been insane, that she had been driven to madness by the bizarre gifts and abilities that she possessed. No one had been able to help Mary but he believed that Stevens could help Lurancy Vennum. He didn't want to see what had happened to his girl happen to someone else's daughter, and so he had brought Dr. Stevens to Watseka in order for him to examine Lurancy.

When they arrived at the house that afternoon, Dr. Stevens found Lurancy sitting in the kitchen next to the stove. She had her feet curled up under her on the chair. Her chin was in her hands and her elbows rested on her knees. She was slumped over, staring at the stove as though entranced by something in the dancing flames that burned inside it. Mrs. Vennum spoke to her but she did not respond. She remained with her eyes fixed straight ahead, as if she was unaware of anyone else in the room.

Dr. Stevens tried to speak to her but she continued to ignore him. Finally, he grabbed one of the chairs that surrounded the kitchen table and pulled it over next to the girl. Lurancy's head snapped around in his direction and she savagely warned him not to come any closer to her. Stevens raised his hands in surrender but he did sit down, his chair a short distance from the one where Lurancy sat. He introduced himself and offered his hand to her in greeting but Lurancy refused to take it. When her parents reprimanded her for being rude, she snapped at them, calling her father "Old Black Dick"

and her mother, "Old Granny." She had a strange look in her eyes, as if she really did not recognize her parents and when her mother reached out to touch her arm, she quickly jerked away from her. She yelled at everyone to leave her alone.

Stevens refused to move and he continued speaking to Lurancy in a calm, quiet voice. She stared at him sullenly for a time and then suddenly, she smiled and brightened up, as if hearing something that made her happy. She told Stevens that she had just discovered that he was a "spiritual doctor" and that she would answer any questions that he asked her. Stevens and Roff exchanged glances. Everyone present was confused. Dr. Stevens had told Lurancy nothing about himself and there seemed to be no way that she could have known that he was a Spiritualist. He had been introduced as a merely a doctor and yet, somehow, Lurancy had known.

Stevens began by asking her name. She said that she was not Lurancy Vennum but a woman named Katrina Hogan.

Stevens then asked: "How old are you?"
"Sixty-three."
"Where do you come from?"
"Germany."
"How long ago?"
"Three days."
"How did you come?"
"Through the air."
"How long will you stay?"
"Three weeks."

During this dialogue, Lurancy's demeanor had changed. She hunched herself over in the chair and her voice cracked, as though she really was an old woman who was answering the questions that Stevens posed to her. Then, she changed again and she became uncomfortable and guilty-acting. She told Stevens that she was not a woman but a young man whose name was Willie Canning. He explained that he had been a troubled young boy who had lost his life. His spirit was inside of Lurancy. He stated: "I am here now because I want to be."

Lurancy answered every question that the doctor asked of her, going into great detail about the life of Willie Canning. Eventually, she seemed to tire of the questions and turned to the doctor and began asking questions of her own, such as "where do you live? Are you married? Do you have children? What kind of doctor are you? Why did you come to Watseka?" This went on for a time and Stevens answered her as best he could, describing his home and life and travels that he had taken around the country. He believed that the questions that he was asked about his travels showed a greater knowledge of geography than Lurancy would have known for her age. Unfortunately, though, much of this session was not recorded by Dr. Stevens, except in very general details.

Lurancy soon took on a sort of devious tone to her voice and her questions changed. She began asking questions about the doctor's habits and morals, questioning him about whether he lied, stole, swore, attended church, prayed and more. She then asked the same questions to be put to Mr. Roff and Mr. Vennum. She declined to ask them directly but forced Stevens to ask them on her behalf. As the other two men answered the questions, Lurancy made "some very unpleasant retorts," Dr. Stevens later wrote.

The situation continued for nearly an hour and a half and then Lurancy began to grow quiet and sullen, refusing to talk or answer any questions that Dr. Stevens asked of her. This went on for several minutes and then, perhaps believing that the girl was now too tired to continue, Stevens got up from his chair to leave. As he did so, Lurancy also stood up. Almost immediately, her hands fluttered in the air and her eyes rolled back into her head. Lurancy's body stiffened and she fell, crashing to the hard wooden floor. Her body was rigid and stiff and it appeared that she had gone into another of her mysterious trances.

Dr. Stevens later stated that he had seen this kind of trance before, describing how "sensitives" fall under the "power of God" during religious revival meetings. He believed that he could restore the senses of such power by "magnetizing" them, which was a form of mesmerism or hypnotism. He explained to the Vennums that he could do the same thing with Lurancy.

Mr. Vennum and Mr. Roff managed to get Lurancy back into her chair and Dr. Stevens sat down in front of her again. He managed to pry her hands, which were stiffly held against her chest, away from her body and took them into his own. His voice lowered to a soft, even tone and he began to speak to her, stroking her hands and easing her from out of the control of the spell. Soon, Lurancy's voice became her own and she began to speak to Dr. Stevens, maintaining that while her body was in the Vennum house, her consciousness was in heaven, where she was conversing with angels.

In this hypnotized condition, Lurancy answered the doctor's questions and spoke of her seemingly insane condition and the influences that were controlling her. She told him that she regretted allowing some of the spirits around her to take control over her body, stating that Katrina Hogan and Willie Canning were evil and forced her to do and say horrible things. Stevens explained to her that she was able to control what spirits influenced her and then asked her that, if she was going to be controlled by spirits, wouldn't it be better to be controlled by a happier, more intelligent and rational being? Lurancy agreed that this would be preferable if she could do it.

Lurancy sat for several minutes in eerie silence. By this time, the winter sun had long since set and the Vennum kitchen was only dimly lighted by the fire from the stove and one kerosene lamp that had been placed on the table. The lengthening shadows danced across the room as Lurancy waited, then let out a long sigh before she spoke again. She said that she had looked about, and had inquired of those around her, to find someone who would prevent the cruel and insane spirits on the other side from returning to annoy her and her family.

She said: "There are a great many spirits here who would be glad to come."

Lurancy proceeded to give names and descriptions of people that Dr. Stevens wrote were "long since deceased" and who were unknown to the girl but often recognized by the older people who were present. Lurancy waited for several more minutes and then explained that she had found one spirit who wanted to come with her. The spirit was a young woman who believed that she could help Lurancy in a way that no other spirit could.

Dr. Stevens asked her the name of the spirit and her whispered reply echoed in the kitchen. Lurancy spoke: "Her name is Mary Roff."

The Coming of Mary Roff

While the name of Mary Roff may have sent shivers down the spines of the adults who were present, the name meant nothing to Lurancy herself. She had never heard of the girl and could not have known what had happened to her years before. Even if we take into consideration that rumors may have circulated about the Roff family and the crazy daughter that they once had who was locked up in an asylum and died, it's likely that Lurancy would not have been exposed to them. The Roff and Vennum families had never had any real contact with one another and Lurancy had been a very young child when Mary had died.

Asa Roff soon recovered from the surprise of hearing his daughter's name on Lurancy's lips and he quickly assured the girl that Mary had been a good and intelligent young woman and would certainly help her in any way that she could. He added that Mary had once suffered an affliction much like the one that was now bothering Lurancy.

Silence again filled the kitchen as Lurancy's unconscious mind deliberated about Mary's presence. Finally, she agreed that Mary would take the place of the troubled and disturbed spirits who had initially possessed her body.

Dr. Stevens and Mr. Roff retired from the house a few hours later. Dr. Stevens wrote: "Leaving the family satisfied that a new fountain of light and source of help had been reached. A new beam of truth reached and touched the hearts of the sorrowing family. And to use the language of Mary Roff, 'Dr. Stevens opened the gate for her,' and for the inflowing light where before was darkness."

Lurancy remained in her trance for the rest of the evening and into the next day. During this time, Lurancy claimed to be Mary Roff.

She was not a spirit inhabiting another girl's body; she insisted that she actually was Mary! She claimed that she had no idea where she was, unable to recognize the Vennum house, which was a place where "Mary Roff" had never been. She wanted to go home, she said, which meant back to the Roff house.

Lurancy was so insistent about this that on the following morning, Friday, February 1, Thomas Vennum called at the office of Asa Roff and explained to him what was happening. He said that his daughter continued to claim that she was Mary and demanded that she be allowed to go home. Vennum said: "She seems like a child real homesick, wants to see her pa and ma and her brothers."

The Vennums had mixed feelings about these latest developments. They were happy to see that the rigid, corpse-like spells, excruciating pain and weird trances had passed but now they had a girl who seemed to be a stranger on the hands. She was very polite, mild and docile but she was constantly begging the Vennums to let her go home. They tried to convince her, as did Mr. Roff, that she was already at home but the girl was having none of it. She would not be pacified. The Vennums were becoming more and more convinced that this girl was no longer their daughter.

The news of this new development quickly spread and when Mrs. Roff heard what had happened, she hurried to the Vennum house in the company of her married daughter, Minerva Alter. The two women hurried up the sidewalk of the Vennum house and saw Lurancy sitting by the window. When she saw them coming, she cried out: "Here comes Ma and Nervie!" As they came into the house, she desperately hugged and kissed the two surprised women and wept for joy. No one had called Minerva by the nickname "Nervie" since Mary's death in 1865.

From this time on, Lurancy seemed more homesick than before, frantically wanting to leave and go home with the Roffs. It now seemed entirely possible to everyone involved that Mary Roff had taken control of Lurancy. Even though the girl still looked like Lurancy Vennum, she knew everything about the Roff family and she treated them as her loved ones. The Vennums, on the other hand, were treated very courteously but she was distantly polite with them, as though living and speaking with strangers. The Vennums were understandably shocked and unnerved by the turn of events. Their daughter had become someone completely unknown to them.

Finally, some friends of the family insisted that the Vennums allow the girl to go with the Roffs for a time. The Vennums were reluctant to do so. They were still befuddled and stunned by what was going on and they also felt that it would be an imposition to send their daughter to be cared for by strangers, no matter who she claimed to be.

After a few more days of the girl's weeping and crying, they decided to discuss the situation with the Roffs. It was a delicate problem but one that Mr. And Mrs. Roff agreed to take on. Braving the ridicule of people in town, and with no other motive but one of kindness, they opened their home to receive Lurancy.

On February 11, Lurancy --- or rather "Mary" --- was allowed to go to the Roff home. The Vennums agreed that this arrangement would be for the best, for now, although they desperately hoped that Lurancy would regain her true identity. The Roffs, meanwhile, saw the possession as a "miracle," as though Mary had returned from the grave. They took Lurancy across town and as they were taking the buggy ride, they passed by the former Roff home, where they had been living when Mary died. The home now belonged to Minerva and her husband, Henry Alter. The girl demanded to know why they were not stopping there and the Roffs had to explain that they had moved several years before to their brick home on Fifth Street. The young woman's lack of knowledge about this move, as well as her identification of the old house, was further proof to the Roffs that Lurancy had been possessed by the dead girl.

Lurancy's arrival in the Roff home, as Mary, was met with great excitement. She immediately began calling the Roffs "ma and pa" and recognized each member of the family. Even though Lurancy knew none of them herself, she greeted them, as Mary, with love and

The Asa Roff home as it looks today in Watseka. This was the second home that the Roffs owned in the city and one that was unfamiliar to Mary, since the family had moved to the house after she had died. The original Roff home became the residence of daughter Minerva, and her husband, Henry Alter.

affection. One of them asked her how long she would stay and she replied: "The angels will let me stay until some time in May."

For the next several months, Lurancy lived as Mary and seemed to have forgotten her former life. As the days passed, however, Lurancy continued to show that she knew more about the Roff family, their possessions and their habits than she could have possibly known if she had been merely faking the whole thing. Many of the incidents and stories that she referred to had taken place years before Lurancy had even been born. Her physical condition began to improve while staying with the Roffs and she no longer suffered from the attacks that had plagued her.

She was happy and quite contented while living in the Roff home and she recognized and called by name many of the neighbors and family friends known to Mary during her lifetime. In contrast, she claimed not to recognize any family members, friends or associates of the Vennums. Even though the Vennums allowed their daughter to live with the Roff family, they did ask her to visit them as often as possible. Lurancy, while living as Mary, came often in the company of

Mrs. Roff and she soon learned to love these "strangers" as friends.

Her day-to-day life in the Roff home was anything but unusual. She was easygoing, affable and hard working, helping with the household chores, cooking and cleaning and going about the activities of any young girl of the time. She liked to read and sing, as Mary always had, and loved sitting with her father and talking about anything that came to her mind. One day she asked him: "Pa, who was it that used to say 'confound it'?" She began laughing when she realized that the saying was one that he often used when Mary was a young girl --- nearly 20 years before.

One day, she met an old friend and neighbor of the Roffs, who had been a widow when Mary was a girl. Some years after Mary had died, the widow had married a Mr. Wagoner but this seemed to be unknown to the girl. When the two were reunited, Lurancy hugged her tightly and called her by the last name of her late husband. She did not seem to be able to comprehend that this family friend had remarried.

A few weeks after Lurancy was settled into the Roff home, Mrs. Parker, who lived next door to the Roff family in Middleport in 1852, and next door to them in Watseka in 1860, came to the house with her daughter-in-law, Nellie Parker. Lurancy, or Mary, recognized both women immediately, calling Mrs. Parker "Auntie Parker," and the other "Nellie," just as she had known them years before. Mary sat down to speak to the two ladies and right away, she asked Mrs. Parker, "Do you remember how Nervie and I used to come to your house and sing?"

Mrs. Parker said that she did and she would later recall this incident and swear that no one had mentioned this to Lurancy before her visit. The young girl had brought up the singing on her own. She testified that Mary and Minerva often visited her house and loved to sing "Mary had a Little Lamb." Minerva also recalled doing this and added that they came to Mrs. Parker's house during the time when Mr. Roff was the postmaster, and not later than 1852. This would have been more than a decade before Lurancy Vennum was born.

One evening in late March, Mr. Roff was reading the paper and having tea and asked his wife if she could find a certain velvet head dress that Mary had worn before she had died. If she knew where it was, he asked her to place it on the stand and say nothing of it, but to wait and see if Lurancy recognized it. Dorothy Ann quickly found the piece and placed it where she had been instructed. Lurancy was outside at the time this took place but she soon came in the door and glanced over as she passed the stand. She immediately exclaimed: "Oh, there is my head-dress that I wore when my hair was short!"

Lurancy took the velvet piece from the stand and lovingly caressed it. The Roffs were both pleased and amazed, seeing this as further evidence that the spirit of Mary was alive within the body of this young girl. It was yet another thing that Lurancy could not have known anything about, and such a trivial matter that even the most clever hoaxer could not have uncovered it as she prepared to fool the family. But Lurancy, or Mary, was not finished yet.

She turned to Mrs. Roff: "Ma, where is my box of letters? Have you got them yet?"

Mrs. Roff found a box filled with letters that had been saved after Mary had died. They were the same letters that Mary had been able to read blindfolded during the eerie tests that she had been subjected to by her father, the ministers and the newspapermen.

Lurancy began to examine them: "Oh, Ma, here is the collar I tatted! Why did you not show to me my letters and things before?"

The collar had been preserved among the things that had been saved as mementoes of a lost child and it was one of the beautiful things that had been created by Mary's hands long before Lurancy had even been born. Like so many other things from her childhood, the spirit of Mary recognized it and spoke of it through the voice and body of another girl. The Roffs needed no further convincing. This was their daughter Mary, no matter what form she might be in at that time.

Of course, not everyone in Watseka believed that Lurancy had been possessed by the spirit of Mary Roff. The Vennums' minister,

The Reverend Baker, after learning that Lurancy was staying with the Roffs, pleaded with the family once again to have the girl committed to the state asylum. He told them: "I think you will see the time when you will wish that you had sent her to the asylum." Others in the congregation shared his thoughts as he added: "I would sooner follow a girl of mine to the grave than have her go to the Roffs' and be made a Spiritualist."

Several of the doctors who had attempted to treat Lurancy started scathing rumors about Dr. Stevens and dismissed the case as nothing more than catalepsy and "humbug." They believed that Lurancy was faking the whole thing and making fools of her parents and the Roff family. Of course, no one who publicized these opinions in Watseka had actually visited either family and had no in-depth knowledge of the situation. This ignorance did not stop the rumors from being spread, though, and the Roffs and Vennums were ridiculed by many in the community. For the most part, they ignored the laughter and the disdain, believing that something truly authentic and supernatural was taking place.

Dr. Stevens continued to play an important role in the case and he visited Watseka often, staying with the Roff family and investigating the phenomenon of Lurancy and Mary. When he returned to Janesville, he was kept in touch with the strange happenings through a series of letters that were sent from Asa Roff, Minerva Alter and from Lurancy, writing as Mary. Portions of these letters are relevant to the mysteries of the case and they are quoted here.

From Asa Roff, February 19, 1878:

You know how we took the poor, dear girl Lurancy (Mary). Some appreciate our motives, but the many, without investigation and without knowledge of the facts, cry out against us and against that angel girl. Some say she pretends; others that she is crazy; and we hear that some say it is the devil.

Mary is perfectly happy; she recognizes everybody and everything that she knew when in her body twelve or more years ago. She knows nobody nor anything whatever that is known to Lurancy.

Mr. Vennum has been to see her, and also her brother Henry, at different times, but she don't know anything about them. Mrs. Vennum is still unable to come and see her daughter. She has been nothing but Mary since she has been here, and knows nothing but what Mary knew. She has entered the trance once every other day for some days. She is perfectly happy. You don't know how much comfort we take with the dear angel.

Lurancy often stated that she loved Dr. Stevens second only to her father (meaning Mr. Roff) because he had done so many kind things for her. He had opened the gate for her to return to life, had provided comfort for her family, and was helping to heal Lurancy's body. Because she was so grateful, she received the Roffs' permission to write to him. Her first letter was dated February 20, 1878:

I am yet here. Frank is better. Nervie is here for dinner; Allie Alter is going to stay the night; Mrs. Marsh was here today and read a beautiful letter to us. I wish you could spend the evening with us. I would like to have your picture to look at. Please write to pa when you get time. We all send our love to you. I like it here very much, and am going to stay all the time. I went to heaven and stayed about an hour. It seems a long time since I saw you.
Forget me not. Good night.
Mary Roff

She wrote to the doctor again on February 21. This is an excerpt from that letter:

I have just finished a letter to brother Frank. He went back to his store feeling quite well. The boys have gone out to play for a dance. In the evening, I went to heaven, and I saw some of the beautiful things, and talked with angels, and be sure I don't forget them when I got to heaven and come back. 'Fear the Lord, depart from evil.' Proverbs 3:7

Mary Roff

As noted in her letter, Lurancy (or Mary) was able to slip into trances and go to the other side, where she spoke to the spirits. However, on occasion, some of those spirits reportedly returned with her and Lurancy acted as a spirit medium would, allowing them to communicate through her. In March, Asa Roff sent a letter to Dr. Stevens, detailing an incident that occurred at one of these impromptu séances:

A lady came through at our house, who claimed to have lived and died in Tennessee, and she says that she was afflicted from eight years of age till twenty-five, when she died with a similar disease, and in a similar way that Mary died. She says that Mary has control of Lurancy Vennum, and will retain control till she is restored to her normal condition, when Mary will leave.

Mary is happy as a lark and gives daily, almost hourly, proofs of being Mary's intelligence. She don't recognize Lurancy's family or friends at all. She knows and recognizes everything that our Mary used to know, and nothing whatever of what the Vennum girl knows. She now enters the trance without any rigidity of the muscles whatever, very gently, and at her own will, describes heavenly scenes, etc. We think all will be well, and Lurancy restored to her orthodox friends yet.

Some of the relatives are yielding by calling Mary's attention to things of thirteen years ago, that transpired between her and them. It wakes them up. It is wonderful. It would take a volume to give the *important items that have occurred.*

Minerva Alter wrote a letter to Dr. Stevens on April 16, 1878:

My angel sister says that she is going away from us again soon, but says she will often be with us. She says Lurancy is a beautiful girl; says she sees her nearly every day, and we do know she is getting better every day. Oh, the lessons that are being taught us are worth treasures of rare diamonds; they are stamped upon the mind so firmly that heaven and earth shall pass away before one jot or one tittle shall be forgotten. I have learned so much that is grand and beautiful. I cannot express it; I am dumb.

A few days ago, Mary was caressing her father and mother, and they became a little tired of it, and asked why she hugged and kissed them. She sorrowfully looked at them, and said 'Oh, pa and ma! I want to kiss you while I have lips to kiss you with, and hug you while I have arms to hug you with, for I am going back to heaven before long, and then I can only be with you in spirit, and you will not always know when I come, and I cannot love you as I can now. Oh, how much I love you all!'

On May 7, 1878, Lurancy (writing as Mary) included a letter to Dr. Stevens in the same envelope that contained a letter from Asa Roff. She wrote:

Dear Doctor – I thought I would write you. I am at Aunt Carrie's. I am going to take dinner with her. Yesterday, I went and spent the day with Mrs. Vennum. She had a dreadful headache and I rubbed it away. Pa is quite busy in his office today. Ma is feeling a good deal better. I am feeling quite well, except my breast hurts me some today. It commenced hurting me last night. I treat ma in the morning and Nervie at night for hard colds and cold feet. We all went to the Reform Club last Saturday. Aunt Carrie's essay was splendid and very affecting. We all read that letter in the Religio-Philosophical Journal *from your daughter, and liked it very much.*

Mary Roff

In the same envelope was a letter from Mr. Roff, which read, in part:

I want to give you a little scene; time; Monday morning, May 6th; place, A.B. Roff's office, Watseka; present, A.B. Roff at the table writing; Frank Roff at the table at the right of A.B.R.; door behind A.B., and a little to the left; enters unheard the person of Lurancy Vennum; places her arm around the neck of A.B. Roff, kissing him and saying, 'Pa, I am going to visit with Mrs. Vennum today.' A.B. Roff looks around and discovers standing in the door Mrs. Vennum, Lurancy's mother, looking on the scene. The girl then bade an affectionate goodbye to Frank; A.B.R. asks, 'How long will you stay?' She replies, 'Till two or three o'clock.' Mrs. Vennum then said to Mr. Roff: 'If she does not get back at that time, don't get alarmed, we will take care of her.' Exit Mrs. V. and the girl.

You don't know how much my heart aches for that poor mother, yet she is much happier than she was last winter with Lurancy as she was.

On May 7, the day that the preceding letter was written, Lurancy (as Mary) called Mrs. Roff to a private room and there, in tears, informed her that Lurancy Vennum would be coming back soon. She could feel the other girl's spirit returning and she had no idea whether or not Lurancy would be staying or not. If Mary was going to be released from the body, then she hoped that she would have time to see Allie, Minerva and Henry so that she could tell them goodbye. The girl wept as she told these things to Mrs. Roff and it was almost as if, no matter how much she wanted to help Lurancy, Mary didn't want to let go of the earthly form that she had managed to obtain.

The young woman sat down in a chair and over the course of the next few minutes, a battle took place for control of her physical form. Her eyes slowly closed and her face shifted expressions several times before her eyes fluttered open again. The girl, confused, looked wildly about before exclaiming: "Where am I? I have never been here before!"

Lurancy Vennum had returned.

Mrs. Roff sat down next to the girl and held her hand, gently rubbing her arm. She tried to calm the girl: "You are at Mr. Roff's, brought here by Mary to cure your body."

Lurancy burst into tears. "I want to go home!"

Mrs. Roff soothed her and told her that someone would send for her parents. She then asked the girl if she felt any pain in her breast. (Lurancy, or Mary, had been complaining of the pain for a few days, continually holding her left breast and pressing on it with her fingers).

Lurancy looked puzzled for a moment and then seemed surprised when she spoke with some confusion: "No, but Mary did."

Lurancy remained with Mrs. Roff for only a few minutes and then a subtle change seemed to sweep over her body and her features. A quiet humming sound came from the girl's lips and then softly turned into song. It was "We are Coming, Sister Mary," a childhood favorite of Mary Roff's. The dead girl had returned to the body of Lurancy Vennum.

Mary's return was marked by sadness and despondency. Everyone knew that, after the brief return of Lurancy, it was nearly time for her to leave. Over the next two weeks, a battle raged for the control of Lurancy's physical body. At one moment, Lurancy would announce that she had to leave and at the next would cling to her father and cry at the idea of leaving him. She spent nearly every day going from one family member to another, hugging them and touching them at every opportunity. She became increasingly upset with each passing day, weeping at the thought of leaving her "real family."

Dr. Stevens returned to town to have as much contact with Mary as he could before she was gone. He found that over the last two weeks, she seemed to be more aware of not only her past life as Mary Roff but also about the fact that she was masquerading, as it were, in a borrowed form. One day, Stevens asked her: "Do you remember the time you cut your arm?"

Lurancy (or Mary) admitted that she did and she rolled up the sleeve of her dress to show him the scar. She started to speak and then paused and added: "Oh, this is not the arm; that one is in the ground." Then, she went on to describe the spot where Mary had been buried and the circumstances of her funeral.

Dr. Stevens also noted that she began to tell of supernatural incidents that occurred after her death. He wrote:

I heard her tell Mr. Roff and the friends present, how she wrote to him a message some years ago through the hand of a medium, giving him name, time and place. Also of rapping and of spelling out a message by another medium, giving time, name, place, etc. which the parents admitted to be true.

The spirit of Mary, dwelling in Lurancy, seemed also to have held on to the clairvoyant abilities that Mary manifested before her death. One afternoon, Lurancy came to her mother and told her that Mary's brother, Frank, had to be carefully watched over during the coming night. He was going to become very sick and he could die if he was not properly cared for. At the time of this announcement, Frank was feeling just fine and, in fact, was uptown playing in a band that had been put together of the Roff brothers and their friends. That same evening, Dr. Stevens had stopped by to visit the family but then had left by 9:30 p.m.

During the early morning hours, Frank was suddenly afflicted with something like spasms and a terrible chill, which caused him to tremble and shake so badly that he almost fainted. Lurancy rushed into his room and saw the situation exactly as she had predicted it. She told her father: "Send to Mr. Marsh's for Dr. Stevens."

Roff replied: "No, Dr. Stevens in at old town."

Mary shook her head: "No, he is at Mr. Marsh's, go quick for him, pa."

Mr. Roff ran from the house and went next door to the Marsh's. Here, he found Dr. Stevens but by the time the doctor could get dressed and hurry to the Roff home, Lurancy had things well in hand. She had made Mrs. Roff sit down, had provided hot water and cloths for the young man and was doing all that could be done for him. The doctor agreed with her methods and allowed her to continue. Mary's spirit, working through Lurancy, had likely saved the young man's life.

The girl also told Dr. Stevens of seeing some of his deceased children on the other side. There were about Mary's age but had been there longer than she had. She told him that she was with them quite often and even traveled to the doctor's home with them. She correctly described his home in Wisconsin, even though she had never been there, gave the names and ages of his children, and as evidence that she was telling the truth, told the daughter of a supernatural experience that had occurred to Mrs. E.W. Wood, one of the doctor's married daughters. Stevens never revealed the details behind the story but attested to the fact that what Lurancy told him had actually taken place.

Strangely, another daughter of the doctor, Emma Angelia, who had died in 1849, sought through Mary to take control of Lurancy's body and go home with her father to Wisconsin, to visit her family for a week. Mary wanted to do this and even asked the Roffs if they would mind if she went, so that the Stevens family could spend some time with Emma. The Roffs did not think that it was advisable and the matter was dropped.

As more time passed, Lurancy's control over her own body began to slowly return. Mary's spirit would sometimes recede into the manner and memory of Lurancy for a time. It was not enough that Mary's identity was lost, or that Lurancy's personality returned, but it was enough to provide evidence that she was returning to her own body.

On the afternoon of Sunday, May 19, Lurancy was sitting in the parlor with Mr. Roff and Henry Vennum, Lurancy's brother, was seated in a chair in the hallway. Other members of the Roff family waited with him in the corridor. He had come to the house to visit his sister and Roff, based on recent experiences, felt that Lurancy's spirit was near. It soon turned out that he was correct in his assumptions. In a matter of moments, Mary departed and Lurancy took control of her body again. Henry was called in and when he stepped into the room, Lurancy wrapped her arms around his neck, kissed his cheek and burst into tears. She was so happy to see him that Henry started to cry, which caused everyone else in the household to weep along with them.

Mr. Roff asked Lurancy if she would be able to stay with them until someone could go to the Vennum house and bring back her mother. Lurancy answered that she could not, but if her mother were brought over, she would come again and be able to talk with her. Her eyes seemed to waver for a moment and her body shook slightly --- Lurancy was gone.

It was obvious to everyone gathered in the parlor that Mary had returned. When someone asked her where she had gone, she replied: "I have seen Dr. Stevens and he looks as good as ever again." Dr. Stevens had recently returned to Wisconsin and Mary implied that she had gone there to see him during the brief time that Lurancy had control over her body.

Lurinda Vennum was brought to the Roff house within the hour and when she came into the parlor, Lurancy once again regained full control of her body. Mother and daughter embraced one another, kissed and wept until everyone assembled was crying in sympathy. Lurancy stayed for a few minutes and then, as mysteriously as she had gone, Mary Roff returned and Mrs. Vennum was a beloved stranger once more.

Lurancy Vennum Returns

On the morning of May 21, Asa Roff wrote to Dr. Stevens:

Mary is to leave the body of Rancy today, about eleven o'clock, so she says. She is bidding neighbors and friends good-bye. Rancy is to return home all right today. Mary came from her room upstairs where she was sleeping with Lottie, at ten o'clock last night, lay down by us, hugged and kissed us, and cried because she must bid us goodbye, telling us to give all her pictures, marbles and cards, and twenty-five cents Mrs. Vennum had given her, to Rancy, and had us promise to visit Rancy often. She tells me to write to Dr. Stevens as follows:

'Tell him I am going to heaven and Rancy is coming home well.' She says she will see your dear children in spirit-life; says she saw you on Sunday last.

She said last night, weeping, 'Oh, pa, I am going to heaven tomorrow at eleven o'clock, and Rancy is coming back cured, and going home all right.' She talked most lovingly about the separation to take place and the most beautiful was her talk about heaven and her home.

Mary sent word to her sister, Nervie, to come to the Roff house and stay with her for an hour so that she could say goodbye. After that, when Lurancy returned, Nervie was to take the girl to Mr. Roff's office and then he would take her to the Vennums. Mary said: "I will come in spirit as close to you as I can, and comfort you in sorrow, and you will feel me near you sometimes."

As 11 a.m. approached, Mary seemed to fight the idea of leaving and allowing Lurancy to return. Minerva was a little upset with her. She spoke, saying, "Mary, you have always done the things that you said you would, but as I don't understand these things, will you please let Lurancy come back just now, and then you can come again if you want to?"

Mary agreed that she would and kissed her mother and sister goodbye. The girl's eyes rolled back for an instant and immediately, she was Lurancy Vennum again. She found herself walking outside with Minerva, starting toward Mr. Roff's office. Lurancy asked Minerva: "Why Mrs. Alter, where are we going?" The girl then paused for a moment and smiled slightly to herself before she spoke again: "Oh yes, I know, Mary told me."

On the way, they met Mrs. Marsh and Mrs. Hoober, who were the nearest neighbors and some of Mary's closest friends. Lurancy did not recognize either of the women, but she was polite to them and greeted them warmly. When she and Minerva walked on, she remarked: "Mary thinks so much of these neighbors."

She then turned to Minerva, with whom Lurancy had been only slightly acquainted with two years before, and said: "Mrs. Alter, Mary can come and talk to you nearly all the way home, if you want her to, and then I will come back."

Minerva agreed: "I have trusted you in the past, and of course, I would love to talk with my sister."

Mary's spirit enveloped Lurancy again and according to Minerva, the two of them talked about many things and family matters as they walked. As the hour for Mary's departure finally arrived, Lurancy returned. She told Minerva and Mr. Roff that she felt as though she had been asleep for a very long time, yet knew that she had not. She asked Mr. Roff if he would take her home and he immediately agreed to do so.

On May 22, Mr. Roff wrote to Dr. Stevens:

Thank God and the good angels, the dead is alive and the lost is found. I mailed you a letter yesterday at half-past ten o'clock a.m. stating that Mary told us she would go away, and Rancy would return at eleven o'clock on the 21st of May. Now I write you that at half past eleven o'clock a.m., Minerva called at my office with Rancy Vennum, and wanted me to take her home, which I did. She called me Mr. Roff, and talked with me as a young girl would, not being acquainted. I asked her how things appeared to her – if they seemed natural. She said it seemed like a dream to her. She met her parents and brothers in a very affectionate manner, hugging and kissing each one in tears of gladness. She clasped her arms around her father's neck a long time, fairly smothering him with kisses. I saw her father just now (eleven o'clock). He says she has been perfectly natural, and seems entirely well. You see my faith in writing you yesterday morning instead of waiting till she came.

Lurancy returned home to the Vennum house. She displayed none of the strange symptoms of her earlier illness and her parents were convinced that she had somehow been cured, thanks to the intervention of the spirit of Mary Roff. She soon became a healthy and happy young woman, suffering no ill effects from her strange experience. She had no memories of the possession, other than of those things that Mary allowed her to know, and it as if the months that she spent as Mary Roff had never happened at all.

IV. The "Watseka Wonder"

In June 1878, Dr. Stevens returned to Watseka to renew his acquaintance and friendship with the Roff and Vennum families. He was especially curious as to whether or not any of Lurancy's spells or trances had returned and whether Mary Roff had actually managed to cure the girl of her affliction.

On Sunday, June 2, Stevens met with Lurancy and her parents at the house of a friend, who lived about two miles away from the Vennums. Lurancy was introduced to him by her father. She was sure that she had never met the man before and came across as a little shy, as one might expect from a young girl meeting a stranger for the first time. They spoke very little that day and Stevens left the meeting feeling both disappointed that he could learn nothing more from the girl and excited that she truly seemed to have been the victim of a possession. She remembered nothing of meeting the doctor during the time that she was living as Mary Roff.

The next day, June 3, brought him a great surprise. Without any notice to anyone as to where he was going that day, Dr. Stevens stopped unannounced at the home of a friend, a noted attorney in Watseka. As he was entering the gate, Lurancy Vennum walked up beside him and greeted him warmly. The doctor was surprised by her presence, especially as she had seemed so reluctant to talk with him the previous day. Lurancy said: "How do you do, Doctor? Mary Roff told me to come here and meet you. Somehow she makes me feel that you have been a very kind friend to me." Lurancy then went on to deliver a long message that she claimed that she had received from Mary, meant for the doctor to hear.

Dr. Stevens later wrote that since the June 3 meeting, he had seen Lurancy many times and on every occasion, she was very friendly and forthcoming. Something about her demeanor had changed and he was convinced that it was because of the intervention of Mary Roff.

On June 25, Lurancy wrote to Dr. Stevens in Wisconsin:

Dear Doctor,

I am feeling quite well today. I was up to Mrs. Alter's today; she is very well at present. This afternoon I called at Mr. Roff's office, and had quite a long talk with him; but of course it was about the loving angels that you and I know so well. Let them twine around your neck their arms and press upon your brow their kiss. Kiss your loving wife for me, and tell her we shall all meet in heaven if not on earth.

I shall visit Mrs. Roff tomorrow. I shall have my picture taken and send it to you in my next letter. I get up early to take the morning air. I should like to have you write a line to me.

Your friend,

Lurancy Vennum

This was the first letter that Dr. Stevens ever received from Lurancy and he was astounded when he saw it. Having been the recipient of a number of letters from the girl when she was manifesting the personality of Mary Roff, Stevens found that this letter was very different in its makeup and penmanship that the letters that he had gotten, written with the same hand, but signed as Mary. Stevens felt this was further proof of the presence of another personality within the girl's body.

As weeks passed, everyone involved in the case watched very closely to see how Lurancy behaved. Would they see a return of the strange seizures and spells? Would they see the possession by Mary Roff return? We can only imagine the anxiety that must have filled the hearts of the Vennums, and even those of the Roffs, who had come to consider this young girl almost a part of their own family.

On July 9, 1878, Lurinda Vennum posted a letter to Dr. Stevens:

Dear Friend,

Mary L. Vennum is perfectly and entirely well, and perfectly natural. For two of three weeks after her return home, she seemed a little strange to what she had been before she was taken sick last summer, but only, perhaps, the natural change that had taken place with the girl, and except it seemed to her as though she had been dreaming, or sleeping, etc. Lurancy has been smarter, more intelligent, more industrious, more womanly and more polite than before. We give credit of her complete cure and restoration to her family to Dr. E.W. Stevens and Mr. and Mrs. Roff, by their obtaining her removal to Mr. Roff's, where her cure was perfected. We firmly believe that had she remained at home, she would have died, or we would have been obliged to send her to the insane asylum, and if so, that she would have died there, and further, that I could not have lived but a short time with the care and trouble devolving on me. Several of the relatives of Mary Lurancy, including ourselves, now believe that she was cured by spirit power, and that Mary Roff controlled the girl.

Mrs. Lurinda Vennum

On July 10, Asa Roff also sent a letter to Dr. Stevens. He wrote:

Dear Doctor,

Mr. Vennum is out of town, but I have often talked with him, and I know his opinion, often expressed, that Lurancy and her mother would have both died if we had not taken the girl; he gives all credit to yourself and us for it. He believes it was spirit agency that did the work. Lurancy is in perfect health and "much more womanly than before" (so her mother says.) She says she used to romp and play with her brothers, and with the horses, etc. Now she is steady; you can hardly imagine how the dear girl loves those who saved her. She sends you a letter today, but thinks it is a little strange that you have not answered her last letter.

Yours, etc.
A.B. Roff

Lurancy's letter, the last to the doctor that we have record of, read:

I am quite well, and much obliged that you showed my letter to your dear wife. I am sure there is nothing for me to be ashamed of. I was down to Mr. M's store, and he told me how you saved his wife's life, and they appreciate it. Will you want me to give you any description of heaven? I will sometime, when there are but few present. I can't write it for I make so many mistakes. I made a short call to Mrs. Alter's.

Please ask your daughter to write to me. Can't you bring your wife when you come? Poor Mr. Wickersham still lives. We should pity such mortals. My aunt says I know all that has transpired, but none know but the angels and you.

Your friend,
Mary L. Vennum

The Public is Aroused

Needless to say, the people of Watseka had watched with great interest as this curious drama played out in their city. But it was not until three months after the affair had ended that the public at large obtained any knowledge about it. Newspapers in Watseka, and in the surrounding area, had quickly reported the final outcome of the case.

The *Watseka Republican* newspaper wrote:

The meeting with her parents at the home was very affecting, and she now seems to be a very healthy, happy little girl, going about noting things she saw before she was stricken, and recognizes changes that have since taken place. This is a remarkable case, and the fact that we cannot understand such things, does not do away with the existence of these unaccountable manifestations.

The editor for the *Iroquois County Times*, under a banner of "Mesmeric Mysteries" wrote of Lurancy Vennum:

It was hard for even the most skeptical not to believe there was something supernatural about her. If she was not prompted by the spirit of Mary Roff, how could she know so much about the family, people with whom she was not acquainted, and whom she had never visited? No stranger would have suspected her of being the victim of disease, though her eyes were unusually bright.

There are yet numberless mysteries in this world, though science has dissipated many wonders, and philosophy has made plain many marvels. There is much that is unaccountable in the actions of Spiritualistic mediums, and they do many things which puzzle the greatest philosophers. Skeptical and unbelieving as we are, and slight as our evidence has been, we have seen enough to convince us that Spiritualism is not all humbug. The case of Lurancy Vennum, a bright young girl of fourteen years, has been the subject of much discussion in Watseka during the past year, and there is a good deal in it beyond human comprehension...

The first news of the story, outside of local newspapers, came from two articles that were contributed by Dr. Stevens to the August

3 and 10, 1878 issues of the *Religio-Philosophical Journal,* one of the leading Spiritualist newspapers in the United States. In the articles, Stevens discussed the case in great detail, emphasizing the fact that, as of the writing, no return of the ailments, trances and spells had returned to bother Lurancy. Stevens gave it as his unqualified conviction that the spirit of Mary Roff had actually returned to earth during her possession of Lurancy Vennum and had been the instrument of her cure.

But not everyone was as convinced. While Spiritualists were more than willing to believe in the possibility of Lurancy being possessed and healed by Mary's spirit, many members of the general public were not so easily impressed. A number of letters were sent to the *Journal,* insinuating and openly alleging that Dr. Steven's narrative of the case was nothing more than a work of fiction.

The veracity of the Roffs was also attacked. Letters were forwarded to Asa Roff from the editors of the *Journal,* inquiring as to the truthfulness of Stevens' account of what he called "The Watseka Wonder." Some of them merely wanted to hear Roff's side of things but others accused him of collaborating with Stevens to force a hoax on the world.

One writer asked: "Is it a fact, or is it a story made up to see how cunning a tale one can tell?"

Another inquired: "Can the truthfulness of the narrative be substantiated outside of yourself and those immediately interested? Can it be shown there was no collusion between the parties, and no former acquaintance?"

A reader suggested: "It is a pretty big yarn, and there might be some arrangement between the parties, or they themselves deceived."

Another, having read the Stevens articles, remarked: "I confess that I am not of your faith, and I am very doubtful whether newspapers are always embodiments of sacred truths, and I wish that under your hand, as a gentleman, you might confirm to me and other doubting friends, the strange, mysterious and to me, fanciful, statements in those two papers. I wrote wholly to overcome a doubting feeling that exists with myself and friends in regard to that remarkable and wonderful personation."

Roff was indignant over the content of many of the letters he received, including those that were so rude that he never shared their content with anyone. He knew what he and his family had experienced and was convinced of the authenticity of the events. He felt he had no need to defend himself but as a believer in the wonders of Spiritualism, and in defense of his friend, Dr. Stevens, and the reputations of Lurancy and Mary, he wrote a lengthy letter to the editors of the *Religio-Philosophical Journal* that served as his reply to the many critics who attacked him, his family, Dr. Stevens and the Vennums. He noted in the letter: "Persons hereafter writing me, who do not receive an answer to their letters, will seek for the information desired in this article."

His reply to the critics read:

I furnished Dr. Stevens will all the material facts in the case, except such as were within his own knowledge. The history of the Vennum family (and Lurancy's condition up to the time he and I went to see her January 31) I obtained from the members thereof, and the neighbors intimately acquainted with them. The narrative, as written by Dr. Stevens, is substantially true in every part and particular, yet the half has not been told, and never can be; it is impossible for pen to describe or language portray the wonderful events that transpired during the memorable fourteen weeks that the girl was at our house. The material facts of the case can be substantiated by disinterested witnesses, whose veracity cannot be questioned and whose evidence would settle any case in a court of law. I refer you to Robert Doyle, Chas. Sherman, S.R. Hawks, Lile Marsh, J.M. Hoober, and their wives, and to Mrs. Mary Wagoner, formerly Mary Lord, all residents of Watseka. As to "collusion," "arrangement," or "ourselves being deceived," that is simply impossible, as you will see if you carefully read the whole narrative over again. I, too, doubt whether newspapers are always "embodiments of sacred truths," but in this case I assure the writer, the Journal *does* embody a very sacred truth, that of man's immortality.

Talking with Mary, we sometimes spoke of her death. She would quickly reply: "I never died" or "I did not die." She never tired of talking of the life beyond this. She would at any time leave her play, her reading or her jovial companions, to talk with her "pa" and "ma" about heaven and the angels, as she termed spirit-life, and spirits that have left the body.

I have questioned Lurancy Vennum on different occasions, as to whether she remembered anything that occurred during the time that Mary had control of her organism, and she states that a very few things occurring the last month that she was controlled, she recollects, but that in all cases the information was imparted by Mary.

In conclusion, let me say to those who doubt or disbelieve the "strange, mysterious and wonderful story." Call to mind Lurancy's condition at her home last January, surrounded with all the kind care of parents, friends and physicians, everything done to alleviate her suffering and perform a cure that human minds and hands could possibly do, yet growing continually worse (if that were possible,) given up by her physicians, her friends, without a ray of hope, the insane asylum ready to receive her, a condition terrible to behold! Then view her condition from May 21 until today, over three months, a bright, beautiful, happy, healthy girl, and then tell me what produced the change. The narrative furnishes the facts; account for them if you can on any other hypothesis, than power exercised through or by the spirit of Mary Roff having control of Lurancy's body.

I am now sixty years old; have resided in Iroquois County thirty *years, and would not sacrifice what reputation I may have by being party to a publication of such narrative, if it was not perfectly true. If any should desire testimonials of my standing, Col. Bundy has some to use as he deems best.*

Asa Roff
Watseka, Ill. August 23, 1878

The letter appeared in the August 31 edition of the *Journal* and the editors followed it with a number of statements as to the reputation of Asa B. Roff. The writers of these testimonials included Matthew H. Peters, the mayor of Watseka; Charles H. Wood, a former judge of the Twentieth Circuit of Illinois; O.F. McNeill, a former county judge; O.C. Munhall, the Watseka postmaster; attorney Robert Doyle; attorney John W. Riggs; Henry Butzow, circuit clerk; Thomas Vennum (not Lurancy's father), who was the former circuit clerk; Franklin Blades, a judge on the Eleventh Judicial Circuit, and former county judge M.B. Wright.

The letters were followed by an announcement from Colonel J.C. Bundy, the editor of the *Journal.* He wrote to the effect that he had "entire confidence in the truthfulness of the narrative, and believes from his knowledge of the witnesses that the account is unimpeachable, in every particular." As for Dr. Stevens, Colonel Bundy stated that he had been personally acquainted with the physician for many years and had "implicit confidence in his veracity."

After all of this, accusations of perjury and deception were obviously futile and aside from saying that it was simply "fraud" (which no one could explain), there were no adequate interpretations for the events that took place in Watseka. There was an increasing tendency to accept the view advanced by those who had participated in the affair.

But not everyone was so inclined, as the people of Watseka would find out a few years later.

The Society for Psychical Research Investigates

In 1890, controversial psychical researcher Richard Hodgson came to Watseka. Prior to this, Hodgson had made a name for himself in the field, especially concerning research into famed psychic medium Leonora Piper. It was during these investigations that Hodgson heard about the events in Watseka and came to Illinois to study them further.

Richard Hodgson is believed to be the first full-time, salaried psychical researcher. During more than 20 years of research, Hodgson moved from skeptic and debunker to a staunch believer in psychic phenomena and the paranormal. Hodgson was born in Melbourne, Australia, on September 24, 1855 and attended college there, receiving several degrees. He moved to England, where he attended Cambridge, and after taking honors in 1881, he began teaching poetry and philosophy. While at Cambridge, he joined an organization called the Cambridge Society for Psychical Research, which was started in 1879 and was a forerunner of the Society for Psychical Research (SPR). The SPR became widely known as the first established group that investigated psychic phenomena.

Hodgson took an active part in the society, exposing a number of fraudulent mediums. When the SPR formed in 1882, Hodgson became one of the first members. He was asked by the SPR to travel to India and investigate the Theosophical Society and its leaders, including Madame Helena Blavatsky. After more than four months in India, Hodgson concluded that Blavatsky was a fraud. A bitter controversy resulted from this with the Theosophists claiming that Hodgson did not understand the psychic phenomena connected to Blavatsky's mediumship and that he was too harsh in his judgment.

This investigation had interested Hodgson in conjuring, and he soon made a name for himself as one of the SPR's most knowledgeable members when it came to sleight of hand tricks and illusions. His work with S.J. Davey to duplicate the slate-writing of the medium William Eglinton continues to be cited as an excellent study of misdirection. Davey worked with Eglinton for awhile and then branched out on his own, finding that he had no trouble convincing audiences that his tricks were actually paranormal events. He and Hodgson made a systematic study, comparing what Davey did to what sitters at his séances claimed to see. They were able to show how unreliable eyewitness testimony can sometimes be. Author and psychical researcher William

Richard Hodgson

James considered their report "the most damaging document concerning eyewitness evidence that has ever been produced."

William James himself was keenly interested in psychic phenomena and was at the center of the SPR's sister society in America, the ASPR, which had been started in Boston in 1885. The society always seemed to be short of keen investigators and funds, so James appealed to the SPR for help. In 1887, Hodgson moved to Boston to assist and became invaluable as the executive secretary. He also took over from James the research management of the extraordinary mental medium Leonora Piper. James had been astounded with the work that he had done with Piper and believed her to be an authentic, gifted psychic. Hodgson was not convinced and he began a regular recording of her séances and even hired private detectives to have her followed.

His opinion of her soon changed. He wrote: "During the first few years, I absolutely disbelieved in her power. I had but one object, to discover fraud and trickery, of unmasking her. Today, I am prepared to say that I believe in the possibility of receiving messages from which is called the world of spirits. I entered the house profoundly materialistic, not believing in the continuance of life after death;

Medium Leonora Piper convinced Richard Hodgson (and many other investigators) about the validity of the spirit world.

today I say I believe. The truth has been given to me in such a way as to remove from me the possibility of doubt."

Hodgson experienced hundreds of sittings with Piper and published two reports about her work, stating that he believed that "survival after death" was the most reasonable interpretation of the results obtained by her séances. This conclusion astonished many of his friends, who had expected him to unmask Piper, as he had done Blavatsky, Eglinton and other mediums. Hodgson, however, became one of many psychical researchers who became convinced of the validity of the paranormal after being exposed to Leonora Piper's mediumship.

But was it only Leonora Piper who convinced him of life after death? Or could one of the key elements in his conversion been his trip to Watseka in 1890?

In April of that year, Hodgson was in the midst of his investigations into Leonora Piper and was not yet convinced that the abilities that she seemed to manifest were genuine. He got sidetracked by the story of the "Watseka Wonder" and decided to travel to Illinois and organize a rigorous investigation into the incident. When he arrived, he found that several of the key participants in the case were unavailable. Dr. Stevens had died and Lurancy had married and moved to Kansas with her husband. However, Hodgson was able to interview Asa Roff, Minerva Alter and a number of friends and neighbors who had first-hand knowledge about the possession.

Hodgson found that the witnesses were completely cooperative and all of them freely answered his questions, reiterating the facts that were given in Dr. Stevens' articles, and adding more information that had been made public. He spent several days in Watseka, going over and over the case. Although Hodgson knew that he had to be careful of unconscious exaggeration and misstatement, he nevertheless deemed the evidence presented to him to be too strong to be dismissed or explained away by ordinary means. The skeptic and debunker had been swayed by the convictions of the people in Watseka and Hodgson believed that they had been touched by something that was beyond the ordinary. He wrote in a report:

I have no doubt that the incidents occurred substantially as described in the narrative by Dr. Stevens, and in my view the only other interpretation of the case -- besides the spiritualistic-- that seems at all plausible is that which has been put forward as the alternative to the spiritualistic theory to account for the trance-communications of Mrs. Piper and similar cases, viz., secondary personality with supernormal powers. It would be difficult to disprove this hypothesis in the case of the Watseka Wonder, owing to the comparative meagerness of the record and the probable abundance of "suggestion" in the environment, and any conclusion that we may reach would probably be determined largely by our convictions concerning other cases. My personal opinion is that the "Watseka Wonder" case belongs in the main manifestations to the spiritualistic category.

Hodgson followed up his report with an article that he wrote for the *Religio-Philosophical Journal* in December 1890 that contained an account of his inquiry and of the additional information that had been brought to light. He concluded his investigation into the case and stated that it was "unique among the record of supernormal occurrences" and freely admitted that he could not "find any satisfactory interpretation of it except the spiritualistic."

The Aftermath of the Watseka Wonder Case

Lurancy remained in touch with the Roff family for the rest of her life. Although she had no real memories of her time as Mary, she still felt a curious closeness to them that she could never really explain. On January 1, 1882, Lurancy was married to George Binning, a farmer who lived about three miles west of Watseka, and in 1884, they moved west to Rawlins County, Kansas, in the northwestern corner of the state.

The Roffs visited with Lurancy often, even after she was married, and saw her at least once each year after she moved to Kansas. Whenever she returned home to Watseka to see her parents, she always stayed with the Roffs for part of the time. During these visits, she would allow Mary to take control of her, just as she did when living with them in 1878.

Aside from this, Lurancy had little occasion to use the mediumistic skills that she had acquired. Her parents rarely spoke with her on the subject, fearing that it would cause a return of the "spells" that plagued her before she was possessed by Mary. Her husband, George Binning, had no interest in Spiritualism and Asa Roff wrote (rather disapprovingly) that he "furnished poor conditions for further development in that direction." This, combined with her household chores and care of her children, made her spirit possessions and talking with the dead things of the past.

Oddly, Lurancy told the Roffs that she was never sick a day in her life after Mary cured her in 1878.

Lurancy lived in Kansas until the death of her husband when he was in his 50s. After that, she moved to Oklahoma for a time and then eventually settled down in Long Beach, California, in 1910. She died there, at the age of 88, in 1952. She raised 11 children in her lifetime but it was said that none of them knew of her strange time as the

"Watseka Wonder" until they were informed of it after her death by a cousin through marriage.

The Vennum family stayed on in Watseka for many years but after the death of her husband, Thomas, Lurinda Vennum moved to Kansas to live with Lurancy and her grandchildren. Both of the Vennums are buried in Oak Hill Cemetery in Watseka.

(Above) The Vennum family monument in Watseka's Oak Hill Cemetery.

(Below) The grave marker of Thomas Vennum

Dr. Stevens lectured on the "Watseka Wonder" for eight years before dying in Chicago in 1886. He was convinced that what had occurred had been genuine and that Mary Roff had actually taken over the body of Lurancy Vennum for a time.

Minerva Alter wrote a short follow-up article to Dr. Stevens' accounts in 1908, when she was 64 years old. In it, she stated that neither she nor her family had any interest in deceiving or misleading people. She vowed the possession had been real, and talked about the

The Roff family monument in Oak Hill Cemetery

The grave marker of Mary's beloved sister,

great joy that she and her parents had felt when they were reunited with a daughter and a sister who had been dead for 12 years. At the time of the writing, she stated that Lurancy was a healthy, middle-aged woman with 11 children, respected as a neighbor and honored as a friend. She added: "Of the part she played in a great drama staged by heaven and earth, and of what she experienced, she has but a dim remembrance."

Asa and Dorothy Ann Roff received hundreds of letters, from believers and skeptics alike, after the story of the possession was printed in newspapers and appeared in magazines all over the country. In 1879, Roff was elected as justice of the peace in Watseka but resigned the position in June of that same year. Without much explanation, he moved to Garden City, Kansas, where his sons lived and where the family had invested considerable amounts of money. He invested in farmland but found that the climate was too dry for it to be profitable and moved to Emporia, Kansas, where he and his wife lived for a year. From Kansas, Roff moved to Council Bluffs, Iowa for two years and then moved to Kansas City, where he lived for several more years.

In 1885, Roff moved back to Watseka and there he and his wife lived the rest of their lives.

The forlorn and weathered grave of Mary Roff

In the spring of 1889, He was elected police magistrate for a term of four years and once more served as justice of the peace. After their deaths, he and Dorothy Ann were both buried in Oak Hill Cemetery.

The grave of Mary Roff rests silently in Oak Hill Cemetery, on the edge of Watseka, just steps away from the final resting places of her parents and her beloved sister, Minerva. For many years, locals made sure that Mary's grave marker was always covered with dirt, for fear that someone might damage or vandalize it in some way. Today, though, the stone is easy to find, although the elements have not been kind and a casual visitor has to look hard to see the young woman's name across the top.

It is here that she rests – this elusive and mysterious enigma of another time and place. Did Mary Roff really return from the grave? And if she did, what dark secrets did she bring with her – and take back again from this side to the next?

V. What Really Happened in Watseka?

The story of the Watseka Wonder remains one of the strangest unsolved mysteries in the annals of American history. What really happened in this small Illinois town in 1878? Did the spirit of Mary Roff really possess the body of Lurancy Vennum? It seems almost impossible to believe but the families of both young women, as well as hundreds of friends and supporters, certainly thought that it happened. One thing is sure --- something extraordinary happened in Watseka involving Lurancy Vennum, her family and the family of a dead girl named Mary Roff. Was it a true spirit possession, a case of mental illness, or the most elaborate and carefully constructed hoax of the 1870s?

The reader will have to decide that for himself but I'll warn you, keep an open mind and be sure to explore all of the possibilities. There is much more to the story of the Watseka Wonder than first meets the eye.

The Hoax

By all accounts, Lurancy Vennum had the memories and personality of a young woman who had been dead for more than 12 years. She had knowledge about the other girl's family that no one outside of it could possibly have known. Or did she?

That seems to be the main question asked whenever anyone considers the idea that the Watseka Wonder case might have been a clever fraud. When examining the case from that possibility, we have to leave out the arguments of those who make statements like "I don't believe in that sort of thing, so it couldn't possibly have happened." Asa Roff received many letters of this sort in the months following the publication of Dr. Stevens' articles but arguments of this sort offer no proof. Like those in Watseka who scoffed at the possession in 1878, these arguments normally come from people who have little, or no, knowledge of the case and have done no research into the events to try and understand them.

Even so, an open-minded researcher into the case cannot ignore the possibility of fraud, no matter how unlikely it might seem. The case of a young woman being possessed by the spirit of a dead girl, having all of her memories and retaining none of her own until the possession ended, does stretch the bounds of belief. But could it have actually happened? Of course, it could have, for, to paraphrase Hamlet, there are things possible that have not even been dreamt of in our limited philosophies. But whether or not it did happen is open for debate.

If we examine the case as possible fraud, we first have to look at those involved and their possible agendas:

Lurancy Vennum: If this were a hoax, it would have to have been started by Lurancy, who managed to fool her family, an eminent physician, friends and scores of townspeople. Not to mention, such a stunt would have been unbelievably cruel on her part to take advantage of the Roff family the way that she did. There is nothing about her personality, save for her erratic behavior in late 1877, to suggest that she was anything more than a kind, considerate and well-liked young woman.

Those who have suggested that she hoaxed the affair claim that she did so because she had fallen in love with Frank, Asa Roff's son, and that she pretended to be Mary so that she could move into the Roff home and be close to him. However, it's hard to take this seriously since, to all intents and purposes, Frank considered Lurancy to be his sister Mary reincarnated. He would have had no romantic interest in her and such desperation would have gained very little on the part of Lurancy.

When considering this scenario, or any other scenario involving a hoax on the part of Lurancy, we have to question how she could have been coached so well that she could know the intimate details of the lives of the Roffs in the way that she did. Could this have been possible? Could she have fooled that many people by simply listening to gossip and information about the family? Prior to the beginning of 1878, the Vennums had almost no contact with the Roff family whatsoever. Mrs. Vennum and Mrs. Roff had met one time and Thomas Vennum and Asa Roff were formal acquaintances, on speaking terms, at best. There seems to be no possible way that Lurancy could have acquired the information that she spoke of while being possessed by Mary Roff. There were hundreds of details, friends whom she recognized, small bits of daily life and much more that could not have come from casual conversation. She would have had to have employed a firm of private detectives, plus learned to be a first-rate actress, to be able to pull off an impersonation of Mary Roff.

Asa Roff: The other main suspect when it comes to a hoax is Asa Roff, Mary's father. While possible motives remain a mystery, it's possible that he could have somehow convinced Lurancy, with the help of Dr. Stevens, that she really was Mary Roff. But why? Those who worked to expose the Spiritualist movement as a fraud in the late 1800s claimed that Roff wanted to bring publicity to the movement, even using his own dead daughter to do so. They claimed that he, along with Stevens, would have done anything to turn this into a big story. Of course, in order to do this, he would have to have enlisted the help of Lurancy, her parents, his own family, dozens of neighbors and even some of the most respected men in Watseka and Iroquois County at the time. Again, this seems rather hard to believe. Roff was one of the best-liked men in town in the 1870s, was one of the founders of Watseka and served in a variety of public offices that required general elections. If he had been a fraud, someone would have spoken out against him but no one did. In fact, many went out of their way to sign affidavits and write letters of support for him concerning the events in question.

There have also been suggestions made that Roff may not have purposely hoaxed the events in the case but had been somehow misled into believing they were genuine. Of course, this would have to mean that Lurancy faked the possession and managed to fool Asa Roff. Those who believe this is a possibility state that Roff was obviously gullible since he was an ardent Spiritualist. In my opinion, such statements are hardly useful since the ranks of Spiritualism in the late 1800s included scientists, scholars, authors, and some of the most esteemed individuals of the day.

So, does a hoax seem likely? Not particularly, since it would have to have involved multiple people, hundreds of confederates (the population of Watseka,) and an ongoing series of lies and deceptions. The story of the Watseka Wonder was not a work of fiction, but what really occurred remains to be seen.

Multiple Personality & Power of Suggestion

For those who are not inclined to believe in the possibility that Lurancy was truly possessed by the spirit of Mary Roff, there are other, more scientific possibilities available. Some of these options don't do anything to impeach the truthfulness of the testimony given by Dr. Stevens, the Roffs and the numerous other witnesses.

One of the other options given in the case is that Lurancy manifested a "secondary personality" in addition to her own. While rare, such cases do exist today, although they were largely unheard of in the 1870s. For those who have rejected the idea of spirit possession, this seems a likely alternative and, on the surface, the incident does bear a striking resemblance to such cases. In 1908, the Watseka Wonder case was re-examined and it was at that time that the idea of a "secondary" or "multiple" personality was presented. Author H. Addington Bruce stated: "Recent research has reported these cases in such numbers, which are due to perfectly natural, although often obscure, causes. In these, as the result of an illness, a blow, a shock, or some other unusual stimulus, there is a partial or complete effacement of the original personality of the victim, and its replacement by a new personality, sometimes of radically different characteristics from the normal self."

One of the cases cited, one bearing a resemblance to the Watseka Wonder case is the account of Reverend Thomas Hanna. Following a carriage accident, Hanna, a Connecticut clergyman, completely lost his identity. He had no memory of any events prior to the accident, recognized none of his friends and in fact, couldn't walk, talk, read or write. He had mentally become a newborn child. However, as soon as the rudiments of education were acquired by him once more, he showed himself to be the possessor of an independent and self-reliant personality --- completely separate from his original one. He had absolutely no memory of his previous personality and had become a new person. Eventually, through hypnosis, Hanna was able to recall his vanished self and, fusing the secondary personality with it, to restore himself to the person that he once was.

At that time, it was believed that the secondary personality was able to retain some of the characteristics of the original self, such as the ability to read and write and other aspects of daily life. In this way, Ansel Bourne, an itinerant preacher from Rhode Island, became "metamorphosed" into a man named A.J. Brown and, without any recollection of his former career, family or friends, drifted to

Pennsylvania and began an entirely new existence as a shopkeeper in a small country town.

Another case, studied by Dr. R. Osgood Mason, involved a young woman who was called Alma Z. for privacy reasons. In this situation, she manifested a secondary personality called "Twoey." Dr. Mason reported that this personality spoke in a peculiar child-like and Indian-like dialect and announced that her mission was to cure the broken-down physical body of the original self. Alma's original personality remained completely dormant as long as "Twoey" was in place. In this regard, the case is very similar to that of Lurancy Vennum with the main difference being that "Twoey" – who, by the way, was credited with having seemingly supernatural powers – did not claim to be a returned spirit from the other side.

By using examples like this, many have drawn distinct parallels between the case of the Watseka Wonder and cases like those just mentioned. In the Watseka case, as in the others, we have the loss of the original self, development of a new self, and the enactment of a role by the new personality that is completely opposite that of the original being. The main difference is the character of the personality that replaced Lurancy's original personality. Here, the claim was made that the secondary personality was that of a girl long dead and by way of proof, vivid knowledge of the life, circumstances and behavior of the dead girl was offered. So, how do we explain this? How did Lurancy conjure up a real personality from the inner depths of her mind? How did her mental illness so perfectly create the identity of a girl who had once lived?

Author H. Addington Bruce submitted what he believed was a credible explanation for this: "On this point, considerable light is shed by the discover that in many instances of secondary personality in which no supernatural pretensions are advanced there is a notable sharpening of the faculties, knowledge being obtained telepathically or clairvoyantly; and by the further discovery that it is quite possible to create experimentally secondary selves assuming the characteristics of real persons that have died."

Subscribers to this theory believe that such a creative force is nothing more than suggestion. To prove this, they cite the case of an instance of mediumship in which the medium, an amateur investigator of psychic phenomena, clearly recognized that his spirit possessions were suggested to him by the spectators at his séances. The medium, a Vancouver schoolteacher named Charles Tout, reported that after attending a few séances with friends, he felt the strong need to become a medium himself and assume a foreign personality. Yielding to the impulse, he discovered, much to his amazement, without losing control of his consciousness, he could develop a secondary personality that could be presented as a discarnate "spirit." On one occasion, he took on the part of a dead woman, the mother of a friend who was present, and it was accepted as a genuine case of "spirit control."

On another night, having given several successful impersonations, he suddenly felt sick and weak and collapsed onto the floor. At this point, one of the sitters remarked: "It is father controlling him." Tout went on to write:

And then I seemed to realize who I was and whom I was seeking. I began to be distressed in my lungs, and should have fallen if they had not held my by the hands and let me gently back to the floor. I was in a measure still conscious of my actions, though not of my surroundings, and I have a clear memory of seeing myself in character of my dying father lying in bed and in the room in which he died. It was a most curious sensation. I saw his shrunken hands and face, and lived again through his dying moments; only now I was both myself, in an indistinct sort of way, and my father, with his feelings and appearance.

Tout explained away the occurrence as nothing supernatural but rather the working out, by some half-conscious part of his personality, of suggestions made at the time by members of his circle, or by something from experience.

This case seems to be the exception rather than the rule when it comes to this sort of thing. In most instances, it seems the original personality is completely effaced and no consciousness is retained of the actions of the secondary self. However, researchers do claim that an avenue of sense remains open and makes it possible for hypnotic suggestions to be made to the original personality. In this way, these personalities can be restored and suggestions can be made as to the actions of the dominant personality.

It is here where some believe the solution to the mystery of Lurancy Vennum lies. According to their theory, Lurancy Vennum was the subject of some "psychic catastrophe" (they do not explain what this might have been) and her mind was opened. That is to say that she momentarily lost all knowledge and control of her personality. When that occurred, it made it possible for a secondary personality to emerge, or as with the medium Tout, for suggestions to create that personality for her.

Proponents of this theory feel that Lurancy may have been predetermined to be "possessed" by a ghost. A few days before her first attack, she informed her family that there were people in her room at night, whispering her name. The next night, she was so frightened that she would only rest if her mother came to her bed with her. These notions of ghostly figures proved to be foreshadowing of the coming trouble and possibly provocative of it. They would act as a powerful autosuggestion and Lurancy would be willing to easily accept the idea that she was possessed by the spirit of a dead girl.

And what of the other spirits that came through first? Those who suggest this theory have an answer to that also. They believe that Lurancy was unconsciously looking for a satisfactory self of ghostly origins. First there was the aged Katrina Hogan, then the troublesome and dangerous Willie Canning, both of which she tried and rejected, likely because her young girl's imagination was unable to invest them with satisfactory attributes. From her family, she received no assistance in her strange quest. They, disbelieving in spirits, persisted in seeing her as insane – a suggestion that was not comforting and far from beneficial. But with the intervention of Asa Roff and Dr. Stevens, everything changed. Not questioning the truth of her assertions, they confirmed them and offered her the gift of a ready-made personality.

Mary Roff was a real person, had a real existence, had once had thoughts, feelings and desires. And Mary, they assured the disintegrated Lurancy, could help her to regain all that she had lost. Needless to say, this was an enticing idea for the disturbed young girl and the sooner that Mary could take her over and help her, the better. For knowledge of Mary, of her characteristics, her relationships, friends, and more (theorists believe), it was only necessary for Lurancy to tap telepathically into the reservoir possessed by Mary's family. Here, there would be, besides general information, a wealth of chance remarks, unconscious hints, unnoticed promptings – all of the suggestions that Lurancy needed to assume this new personality. Her shattered psyche, searching for a secondary personality, eagerly took what was offered to her and Lurancy became, at least for a time, Mary Roff.

Theorists also believe that suggestion was instrumental in not only creating Mary's personality, but expelling it and restoring Lurancy to health. If the responsibility for the creation of the spirit lies with Dr. Stevens and the Roffs, then likewise credit belongs to them for the cure. Their insistence on the fact that Mary's spirit could provide a cure for the girl was itself as powerful a suggestion as anything that could be given by a modern practitioner of mental health science. It unconsciously set a limit to the time of the possession and also created the fixed idea that she was not Lurancy Vennum but Mary Roff and in the month of May, she would become Lurancy again. It was as though Stevens and the Roffs had actually hypnotized her and given her commands that were to be obeyed.

When the time came for the transformation, it occurred with some amount of struggle, a period of alternating personality, with Mary in charge at one moment and Lurancy in control at another.

Proponents of the theory that Lurancy was somehow "hypnotized" into believing she was Mary Roff see this as normal and point out that Mary only returned in the future when Lurancy was in the presence of the Roffs.

Mystery solved.

But is it really? Isn't it interesting when theories to debunk a case seem to be more complex, more convoluted and harder to believe than if we simply say "it must have been a ghost?" While the secondary personality theory does have some interesting – and believable – components to it, overall it's still pretty hard to swallow. For one thing, this theory requires us to believe that Lurancy was somehow capable of reading the minds of the Roff family, their relatives, friends and neighbors. This is in spite of the fact that she had never manifested any such ability before, or after, the case. Secondly, we also have to make the leap that Lurancy suffered some sort of psychic trauma that would have caused her personality to split, or for her to assume a secondary one. There is nothing in the records to indicate how, or when, this might have occurred. Since the start of her seizures and spells seemed to take the Vennum family by surprise, it seems likely that there would have been something in the record about her having mental issues prior to this, if they had actually occurred.

In each of the cases cited but those who believe that Lurancy Vennum created Mary as a secondary personality, these alternate personalities were always fictional characters that were created by the victim. Even in the case of the medium Charles Tout, he manifested the "spirit" of his own dead father, a person he knew well. However, Lurancy did not know Mary, had never met her, did not know her family, her friends or anyone connected to her. To try and explain that her in-depth, intimate knowledge of Mary came because she could suddenly "read minds" is a rather ridiculous and lame attempt to explain away the unexplainable. Even a casual reader of this account will see that there was much more to this case than this weak theory can provide.

Could there have been a scientific explanation for what occurred? There certainly could have been, however, no one has been able to find it. Which leaves us with only one more possible explanation for what took place in Watseka...

The Spirit of Mary Roff

Sir Arthur Conan Doyle once wrote for his master detective Sherlock Holmes: "Eliminate the impossible and whatever remains, however improbable, must be the truth." In this case, if we have ruled out the idea that the Watseka Wonder incident was hoax and have rejected the idea that Lurancy created a secondary personality, then what do we have left? All that remains is that in January 1878, Lurancy Vennum became possessed by the spirit of Mary Roff, a girl who had died more than a decade before.

That's what many people believe. Is it the truth? That is, of course, up to you as the reader to decide. As for my own thoughts on this mysterious case? Well, I still don't know. I do believe that something amazing occurred in Watseka in the spring of 1878 and I do believe that it permanently affected not only the Vennum and Roff families, but also the entire town of Watseka itself.

Was Lurancy actually possessed by the spirit of Mary Roff? Logic tells me that it couldn't have happened but this case certainly gives me pause. The story of the "Watseka Wonder" can make just about anyone wonder if we know as much about the unexplained as we think we do.

It certainly inspires that feeling in me.

Bibliography

Blum, Deborah – Ghost Hunters (2006)

Brandon, Ruth - The Spiritualists (1983)

Brown, Slater - The Heyday of Spiritualism (1970)

Bruce, H. Addington – The Watseka Wonder (Sunday Magazine of the *Chicago Record-Herald* – July 14, 1908)

Bruce, H. Addington – Historic Ghosts and Ghost Hunters (1908)

Chambers, Paul - Paranormal People (1998)

Guiley, Rosemary Ellen – Encyclopedia of Ghosts & Spirits (2000)

Iroquois County Times Newspaper

McHargue, Georgess - Facts, Frauds and Phantasms (1972)

Melton, J. Gordon - Ency. of Occultism and Parapsychology (1996)

Moore, L. - In Search of White Crows (1977)

Murphy, Gardner, M.D. & Robert Ballou – William James on Psychical Research (1960)

Oak Hill Cemetery Records

Oesterreich, Traugott – Possession & Exorcism (1974)

Portrait & Biographical Record of Iroquois County, IL 1893 (Chicago; Lake City Publishing Co.)

Reader's Digest Books - Into the Unknown (1981)

Religio-Philosophical Journal (1890)

Survival After Death – Richard Hodgson

Scott, Beth & Michael Norman – Haunted Heartland (1985)

Somerlott, Robert – Here, Mr. Splitfoot (1971)

Stevens, E. Winchester – The Watseka Wonder (1879)

Taylor, Troy – Devil Came to St. Louis (2006)

Taylor, Troy – Haunted Illinois (2004)

Taylor, Troy – Mysterious Illinois (2006)
Wikipedia Online Encyclopedia
1900 Census of Watseka, Middle Township, Iroquois County, Illinois

Personal Interviews & Correspondence

Special Thanks to:

Jill Hand – Editing & Proofreading Services
Iroquois County Historical Society
Staff of the Watseka Public Library
City of Watseka
Scott Anderson – Owner of the Vennum House
John Whitman – Owner of the Roff House
Christopher Booth
Philip Booth
Keith Age
Orrin Taylor
Rosemary Ellen Guiley
& Haven Taylor

Children of the Grave

The Possessed would not have been possible without the assistance of the Booth Brothers, makers of the film Children of the Grave. (October 2007)

The Watseka Wonder will be featured in the sequel to the film:

Children of the Grave 2: The Possessed

Coming in 2008!

www.childrenofthegrave.com

About the Author

Troy Taylor is the author of 52 books about history, hauntings and the unexplained in America for Whitechapel Press and Barnes & Noble Press respectively. He is the founder and president of the American Ghost Society, a national network of ghost hunters.

Taylor was born on September 24, 1966 in Decatur, Illinois, a Midwestern city that is steeped in legend and lore. Even the hospital in which he was born is allegedly haunted by a phantom nun! He grew up fascinated with things that go bump in the night, as well as the writings of haunted travel writer Richard Winer and legendary ghost hunter, Harry Price. In school, Taylor was well-known for his interest in the paranormal and often took friends on informal ghost tours of haunted places all over downstate Illinois. He would later turn this interest into his full-time career.

In 1989, Taylor started working in a bookstore and a few years later, he wrote his first book on ghosts. It was called Haunted Decatur and delved into the ghosts and hauntings of the city where he grew up. He also created a tour that took guests to places that he had written about in the book. The book became an immediate success and its popularity, along with his previous experiences with ghost hunting, established Taylor as an authority on the supernatural. The book and tour led to media and public appearances and numerous requests to investigate ghostly phenomena.

In 1996, Taylor organized a group of ghost enthusiasts into an investigation team and the American Ghost Society was launched, gained over 600 members in the years that followed. The organization continues today as one of America's largest and most honored research groups.

In 1998, Taylor moved his operations, which now included the American Ghost Society, a history and hauntings bookstore and a publishing company called Whitechapel Press, to Alton, Illinois, near St. Louis. In Alton, Taylor started his second tour company, Alton Hauntings, which took guests to local haunted places in the small Mississippi River town. He would go on to put the place on the map as one of the most haunted small towns in America.

Taylor remained in Alton until 2005, when he returned to Decatur. By then, he had also established two more tour companies, in Springfield, Illinois and another company that arranges overnight stays in haunted places called American Hauntings. These tours, including those in Decatur and Alton, were organized under the heading of the Illinois Hauntings Ghost Tours.

In 2006, Taylor also launched the Weird Chicago Tours, which are based on his book, Weird Illinois, which was published by Barnes & Noble Press. In 2007, Illinois Hauntings also launched ghost tours in Lebanon, Illinois and in Jacksonville.

In 2007, Taylor incorporated as Dark Haven Entertainment, Inc., a parent company for Whitechapel Press, the Illinois Hauntings Tours and for the Ghosts of the Prairie Website and Magazine. The new company also handles the film rights to Troy's ghost books and stories. Currently, there are three of his works optioned for possible film and television production.

Along with writing about the unusual and hosting tours, Taylor is also a public speaker on the subject of ghosts and hauntings and has spoken to literally hundreds of private and public groups on a variety of paranormal subjects. He has appeared in newspaper and magazine articles about ghosts and has also been fortunate enough to be interviewed hundreds of times for radio and television broadcasts about the supernatural. He has also appeared in a number of documentary films, several television series and in one feature film about the paranormal.

He currently resides in Central Illinois with his wife, Haven, in a decidedly non-haunted house.

About Whitechapel Press

Whitechapel Productions Press is a division of Dark Haven Entertainment and a small press publisher, specializing in books about ghosts and hauntings. Since 1993, the company has been one of America's leading publishers of supernatural books and has produced such best-selling titles as **Haunted Illinois**, **The Ghost Hunters Guidebook**, **Ghosts on Film, Confessions of a Ghost Hunter, Resurrection Mary, Bloody Chicago, The Haunting of America, Spirits of the Civil War** and many others.

With nearly a dozen different authors producing high quality books on all aspects of ghosts, hauntings and the paranormal, Whitechapel Press has made its mark with America's ghost enthusiasts.

Whitechapel Press is also the publisher of the acclaimed **Ghosts of the Prairie** magazine, which started in 1997 as one of the only ghost-related magazines on the market. It continues today as a travel guide to the weird, haunted and unusual in Illinois. Each issue also includes a print version of the Whitechapel Press ghost book catalog.

You can visit Whitechapel Productions Press online and browse through our selection of ghostly titles, plus get information on ghosts and hauntings, haunted history, spirit photographs, information on ghost hunting and much more. by visiting the internet website at:

www.prairieghosts.com

9 781892 523556